The Blessed Virgin Mary

THE MANY AND ABUNDANT GRACES DISPENSED BY
THE MOTHER OF GOD TO HER DEVOUT CLIENTS.

BY

ST. ALPHONSUS LIGUORI,

*Doctor of the Church, Founder of the Congregation of the
Most Holy Redeemer.*

TAN BOOKS AND PUBLISHERS, INC.
Rockford, Illinois 61105

Nihil Obstat.

THOMAS L. KINKEAD,
Censor Librorum.

Imprimatur.

✝ MICHAEL AUGUSTINE,
Archbishop of New York.

First published in this format in 1974 by Marian Publications, South Bend, Indiana.

Copyright © 1974 Marian Publications.

Copyright © 1982 TAN Books and Publishers, Inc.

ISBN: 0-89555-177-2

TAN BOOKS AND PUBLISHERS, INC.
P.O. Box 424
Rockford, Illinois 61105

1982

PREPARATORY PRAYER

Come, Holy Ghost, fill the hearts of Thy faithful and kindle in them the fire of Thy love.

℣. Send forth Thy Spirit, and they shall be created;

℟. And Thou shalt renew the face of the earth.

Let us pray.

O God, who didst teach the hearts of Thy faithful people by sending them the light of Thy Holy Spirit, grant us by the same Spirit to have a right judgment in all things, and evermore to rejoice in His holy comfort. Through Christ our Lord. Amen

M ost holy Virgin Immaculate, my Mother Mary, to thee who art the Mother of my Lord, the Queen of the universe, the advocate, the hope, the refuge of sinners, I who am the most miserable of all sinners, have recourse this day. I venerate thee, great Queen, and I thank thee for the many graces thou hast bestowed upon me even unto this day; in particular for having delivered me from the hell which I have so often deserved by my sins. I love thee, most dear Lady; and for the love I bear thee, I promise to serve thee willingly for ever and to do what I can to make thee loved by others also. I place in thee all my hopes for salvation; accept me as thy servant and shelter me under thy mantle, thou who art the Mother of mercy. And since thou art so powerful with God, deliver me from all temptations, or at least obtain for me the strength to overcome them until death. From thee I implore a true love for Jesus Christ. Through thee I hope to die a holy death. My dear Mother, by the love thou bearest to Almighty God, I pray thee to assist me always, but most of all at the last moment of my life. Forsake me not then, until thou shalt see me safe in heaven, there to bless thee and sing of thy mercies through all eternity. Such is my hope. Amen (St. Alphonsus M. de' Liguori).

The faithful who recite this prayer with devotion before an image of the B. V. Mary, may gain:

An indulgence of 3 years.

CONTENTS.

CHAPTER I.

Salve Regina, Mater Misericordiæ!

MARY, OUR QUEEN, OUR MOTHER.

CHAPTER II.

Vita, Dulcedo.

MARY, OUR LIFE, OUR SWEETNESS.

CHAPTER III.

Spes nostra ! salve.

MARY, OUR HOPE.

My queen, my mother! I give
myself entirely to Thee.

THE QUEEN OF HEAVEN

THE BLESSED VIRGIN

CHAPTER I.

Salve, Regina, Mater Misericordiæ!

HAIL, HOLY QUEEN, MOTHER OF MERCY!

MARY, OUR QUEEN, OUR MOTHER.

I. How great should be our Confidence in Mary, who is the Queen of Mercy.

As the glorious Virgin Mary has been raised to the dignity of Mother of the King of kings, it is not without reason that the Church honors her, and wishes her to be honored by all, with the glorious title of Queen.

"If the Son is a king," says St. Athanasius, "the Mother who begot Him is rightly and truly considered a Queen and Sovereign."* "No sooner had Mary," says St. Bernardine of Siena, "consented to be Mother of the Eternal Word, than she merited by this consent to be made Queen of the world and of all creatures."† "Since the flesh of Mary" remarks the Abbot Arnold of Chartres, "was not different from that of Jesus, how can the royal dignity of the Son

* *Serm. de Deip.*   † *Pro Fest. V. M.* s. 5, c. 3.

9

be denied to the Mother?" *   " Hence we must consider the glory of the Son, not only as being common to His Mother, but as one with her." †

And if Jesus is the King of the universe, Mary is
also its Queen. "And as Queen," says the Abbot
Rupert, "she possesses, by right, the whole kingdom
of her Son." ‡   Hence St. Bernardine of Siena concludes that " as many creatures as there are who serve
God, so many they are who serve Mary : for as angels
and men, and all things that are in heaven and on
earth, are subject to the empire of God, so are they
also under the dominion of Mary!" §   The Abbot
Guerricus, addressing himself to the divine Mother
on this subject, says : " Continue, Mary, continue
to dispose with confidence of the riches of thy Son ;
act as Queen, Mother, and Spouse of the King: for
to thee belongs dominion and power over all creatures !" ‖

Mary, then is a queen : but, for our common consolation, be it known that she is a Queen so sweet,
clement, and so ready to help us in our miseries, that
the holy Church wills that we should salute her in this
prayer under the title of Queen of mercy.

"The title of queen," remarks Blessed Albert the
Great, ¶ " differs from that of empress, which implies
severity and rigor in signifying compassion and
charity towards the poor." " The greatness of kings
and queens," says Seneca, "consists in relieving the
wretched "; ** and whereas tyrants, when they reign,
have their own good in view, kings should have that
of their subjects at heart. For this reason it is that,

---

* *De Laud. B. Virg.*   † *Ibid.*   ‡ *In Cant.* l. 3.
§ *Pro Fest. V. M.* s. 5, c. 6.   ‖ *In Ass. B. M.* s. 3.
¶ *Super Miss.* q. 162.   ** *Medea, act.* 2.

at their consecration, kings have their heads an-
nointed with oil, which is the symbol of mercy, to
denote that, as kings, they should, above all things,
nourish in their hearts feelings of compassion and
benevolence towards their subjects.

Kings should, then, occupy themselves principally
in works of mercy, but not so as to forget the just
punishments that are to be inflicted on the guilty. It
is, however, not thus with Mary, who, although a
Queen, is not a queen of justice, intent on the pun-
ishment of the wicked, but a queen of mercy, intent
only on commiserating and pardoning sinners. And
this is the reason for which the Church requires that
we should expressly call her " the Queen of mercy."
The great Chancellor of Paris, John Gerson, in his
commentary on the words of David, "These two
things have I heard, that power belongeth to God,
and mercy to Thee, O Lord," * says that the kingdom of God, consisting in justice and mercy, was
divided by Our Lord : the kingdom of justice He reserved for Himself, and that of mercy He yielded to
Mary, ordaining at the same time that all mercies
that are dispensed to men should pass through the
hands of Mary, and be disposed of by her at will.
These are Gerson's own words: " The kingdom of
God consists in power and mercy ; reserving power to
Himself, He, in some way, yielded the empire of
mercy to His Mother." † This is confirmed by St.
Thomas, in his preface to the Canonical Epistles,
saying, "that when the Blessed Virgin conceived the
Eternal Word in her womb, and brought Him forth,
she obtained half the kingdom of God; so that she is
Queen of mercy, as Jesus Christ is King of justice."

* Ps. lxi. 12.　　† *Super Magn.* tr. 4.

The Eternal Father made Jesus Christ the King of justice, and consequently universal Judge of the world: and therefore the Royal Prophet sings: "Give to the King Thy judgment, O God, and to the King's Son Thy justice."* Here a learned interpreter takes up the sentence, and says: "O Lord, Thou hast given justice to Thy Son, because Thou hast given mercy to the King's Mother." And, on this subject, St. Bonaventure, paraphrasing the words of David, thus interprets them: "Give to the King Thy judgment, O God, and Thy mercy to the Queen His Mother." Ernest, Archbishop of Prague, also remarks, "that the Eternal Father gave the office of judge and avenger to the Son, and that of showing mercy and relieving the necessitous to the Mother."† This was foretold by the prophet David himself; for he says that God (so to speak) consecrated Mary Queen of mercy, anointing her with the oil of gladness: "God hath anointed thee with the oil of gladness."‡ In order that we miserable children of Adam might rejoice, remembering that in heaven we have this great Queen, overflowing with the unction of mercy and compassion towards us; and thus we can say with St. Bonaventure, "O Mary, thou art full of the unction of mercy, and of the oil of compassion;"§ therefore God has anointed thee with the oil of gladness.

And how beautifully does not Blessed Albert the Great apply to this subject the history of Queen Esther, who was herself a great type of our Queen Mary!

We read, in the fourth chapter of the Book of Esther, that in the reign of Assuerus a decree was issued, by which all Jews were condemned to death. Mardochai,

---

* Ps. lxxi. 2.   † *Marial.* c. 127.
‡ Ps. xliv. 8.   § *Spec. B. M. V. lect.* 7.

who was one of the condemned, addressed himself to
Esther, in order that she might interpose with Assuerus
and obtain the revocation of the decree, and thus be
the salvation of all. At first Esther declined the
office, fearing that such a request might irritate the
king still more; but Mardochai reproved her, sending
her word that she was not to think of saving only herself, for God had placed her on the throne to obtain
the salvation of all the Jews: "Think not that thou
mayest save thy life only, because thou art in the king's
house, more than all the Jews." * Thus did Mardochai address Queen Esther. And so can we poor sinners address our Queen Mary, should she show any
repugnance to obtain of God our delivery from the
chastisement we have justly deserved: "Think not, O
Lady, that God has raised thee to the dignity of Queen
of the world, only to provide for thy good ; but in order
that, being so great, thou mightest be better able to
compassionate and assist us miserable creatures."

As soon as Assuerus saw Esther standing before him,
he asked her, with love, what she came to seek. "What
is thy request?" The Queen replied, "If I have found
favor in thy sight, O King, give me my people, for
which I request."† Assuerus granted her request, and
immediately ordered the revocation of the decree.
And now, if Assuerus, through love for Esther, granted,
at her request, salvation to the Jews, how can God refuse the prayers of Mary, loving her immensely as He
does, when she prays for poor miserable sinners, who
recommend themselves to her, and says to him, "My
King and my God, if ever I have found favor in Thy
sight" (though the divine Mother well knows that she

* Esth. iv.13.   † Esth. vii. 2, 3.

was the blessed, the holy one, the only one of the human race who found the grace lost by all mankind; well does she know that she is the beloved one of her Lord, loved more than all the saints and angels together), "give me my people for which I ask"? "If Thou lovest me", she says, "give me, O Lord, these sinners, for whom I entreat Thee." Is it possible that God should refuse her? And who is ignorant of the power of the prayers of Mary with God? "The law of clemency is on her tongue." * Each of her prayers is, as it were, an established law for Our Lord, that He should show mercy to all for whom she intercedes. St. Bernard asks why the Church calls Mary "the Queen of mercy." And he replies, that "it is because we believe that she opens the abyss of the mercy of God to whomsoever she wills, when she wills, and as she wills; so that there is no sinner, however great, who is lost if Mary protects him."†

But perhaps we may fear that Mary would not deign to interpose for some sinners, because they are so overloaded with crimes? Or perhaps we ought to be overawed at the majesty and holiness of this great Queen? "No," says St. Gregory VII.; "for the higher and more holy she is the greater is her sweetness and compassion towards sinners who have recourse to her with the desire to amend their lives." ‡ Kings and queens, with their ostentation of majesty, inspire terror, and cause their subjects to fear to approach them: but what fear, says St. Bernard, can the miserable have to approach this Queen of mercy for she inspires no terror, and shows no severity, to those who come to her, but is all sweetness and gentleness. "Why should

---

* Prov. xxxi. 26.   † *In Salve Reg.* s. i.   ‡ *Lib.* i. *Ep.* 47.

human frailty fear to go to Mary ?   In her there is no austerity, nothing terrible : she is all sweetness, offering milk and wool to all."* Mary is not only willing to give, but she herself offers milk and wool to all: the milk of mercy to animate our confidence, and the wool of her protection against the thunderbolts of divine justice.

Suetonius † relates of the Emperor Titus that he could never refuse a favor, so much so that he sometimes promised more than he could grant, and when admonished of this he replied, that a prince should never send away dissatisfied any person whom he admitted to his audience.   Titus spoke thus, but in reality he must often have deceived or failed in his promises. Our Queen cannot deceive, and can obtain all that she wills for her clients.   Moreover, "Our Lord has given her so benign and compassionate a heart," says Lanspergius, "that she cannot send away any one dissatisfied who prays to her." ‡ But how, to use the words of St. Bonaventure, canst thou, O Mary, who art the Queen of mercy, refuse to succor the miserable ?   And "who," asks the saint, "are the subjects for mercy if not the miserable ?   And since thou art the Queen of mercy," he continues, "and I am the most miserable of sinners, it follows that I am the first of thy subjects.   How, then, O Lady, canst thou do otherwise than exercise thy mercy on me ?"§   Have pity on us, then, O Queen of mercy, and take charge of our salvation.

"Say not, O holy Virgin," exclaims St. George of Nicomedia, "that thou canst not assist us on account of the number of our sins, for thy power and thy

---

* *In Sign. Magn.* † Tit. c. 8.
‡ *Alloq.* l. i, p. 4. *can.* 12. § *Paciucch. In Salve Reg. exc.* 2.

compassion are such that no number of sins, however great, can outweigh them.   Nothing resists thy
power, for our common Creator, honoring thee as His
Mother, considers thy glory as His own; " and the Son,
" exulting in it, fulfils thy petition as if He were paying
a debt; " * meaning thereby that although Mary is
under an infinite obligation to the Son for having
chosen her to be His Mother, yet it cannot be denied
that the Son is under great obligation to her for having given Him His humanity; and therefore Jesus, to
pay, as it were, what He owes to Mary, and glorying in
her glory, honors her in a special manner by listening
to and granting all her petitions.

How great, then, should be our confidence in this
Queen, knowing her great power with God, and that
she is so rich and full of mercy that there is no one
living on the earth who does not partake of her compassion and favor.   This was revealed by our blessed
Lady herself to St. Bridget, saying, " I am the Queen
of heaven and the Mother of mercy; I am the joy of
the just, and the door through which sinners are
brought to God.   There is no sinner on earth so
accursed as to be deprived of my mercy; for all, if
they receive nothing else through my intercession, receive the grace of being less tempted by the devils
than they would otherwise have been." " No one,"
she adds, " unless the irrevocable sentence has been
pronounced" (that is, the one pronounced on the
damned), " is so cast off by God that he will not return to Him, and enjoy His mercy, if he invokes my
aid." † " I am called by all the Mother of mercy,
and truly the mercy of my Son towards men has made

* *Or. de Ingr. B. V.*   † Rev. 1. 6, c. 10.

me thus merciful towards them ; " * and she concludes by saying, " And therefore miserable will he be, and miserable will he be to all eternity, who, in this life, having it in his power to invoke me, who am so compassionate to all, and so desirous to assist sinners, is miserable enough not to invoke me, and so is damned." †

Let us, then, have recourse, and always have recourse, to this most sweet Queen, if we would be certain of salvation; and if we are alarmed and disheartened at the sight of our sins, let us remember that it is in order to save the greatest and most abandoned sinners, who recommend themselves to her, that Mary is made the Queen of mercy. Such have to be her crown in heaven; according to the words addressed to her by her divine Spouse: " Come from Libanus, my spouse; come from Libanus, come: thou shalt be crowned ; . . . from the dens of the lions from the mountains of the leopards." ‡ And what are these dens of beasts but miserable sinners, whose souls have become the home of sin, the most frightful monster that can be found? " With such souls," says the Abbot Rupert, addressing our blessed Lady, " saved by thy means, O great Queen Mary, wilt thou be crowned in heaven; for their salvation will form a diadem worthy of, and well-becoming, a Queen of mercy." §

* Rev. l. 2. c. 23.
† Ibid.
‡ Cant. iv. 8.
§ In Cant. l. iii.

Prayer.

O Mother of my God, and my Lady Mary; as a beggar, all wounded and sore, presents himself before a great queen, so do I present myself before thee, who art the Queen of heaven and earth. From the lofty throne on which thou sittest, disdain not, I implore thee, to cast thine eyes on me, a poor sinner. God has made thee so rich that thou mightest assist the poor, and has constituted thee Queen of Mercy in order that thou mightest relieve the miserable. Behold me then, and pity me : behold me and abandon me not, until thou seest me changed from a sinner into a saint. I know well that I merit nothing ; nay more, that I deserve, on account of my ingratitude, to be deprived of the graces that, through thy means, I have already received from God. But thou, who art the Queen of Mercy, seekest not merits, but miseries, in order to help the needy. But who is more needy than I? O exalted Virgin, well do I know that thou, who art Queen of the universe, art already my queen ; yet am I determined to dedicate myself more especially to thy service, in order that thou mayest dispose of me as thou pleasest. Therefore do I address thee in the words of St. Bonaventure: " Do thou govern me, O my Queen, and leave me not to myself."* Command me ; employ me as thou wilt, and chastise me when I do not obey; for the chastisements that come from thy hands will be to me pledges of salvation. I would rather be thy servant than the ruler of the earth. " I am thine; save me."† Accept me, O Mary, for thine own, and as thine, take charge of my salvation. I will no longer be mine ; to thee do I give myself. If, during the time past I have served thee ill, and lost so many occasions of honoring thee, for the future I will be one of thy most

---

* *Stim. div. Am.* p. 3, c. 19.   † Ps. cxviii, 94.

loving and faithful servants. I am determined that from this day forward no one shall surpass me in honoring and loving thee, my most amiable Queen. This I promise; and this, with thy help, I hope to execute. Amen.

II. How much our Confidence in Mary should be Increased because she is our Mother.

It is not without a meaning, or by chance, that Mary's clients call her Mother; and indeed they seem unable to invoke her under any other name, and never tire of calling her Mother. Mother, yes! for she is truly our Mother; not indeed carnally, but spiritually; of our souls and of our salvation.

Sin, by depriving our souls of divine grace, deprived them also of life. Jesus our Redeemer, with an excess of mercy and love, came to restore this life by His own death on the cross, as He Himself declared: "I am come that they may have life, and may have it more abundantly."* He says more abundantly; for, according to theologians, the benefit of redemption far exceeded the injury done by Adam's sin. So that by reconciling us with God He made Himself the Father of souls in the law of grace, as it was foretold by the prophet Isaias: "He shall be called the Father of the world to come, the Prince of Peace."† But if Jesus is the Father of our souls, Mary is also their Mother; for she, by giving us Jesus, gave us true life: and afterwards, by offering the life of her Son on Mount Calvary for our salvation, she brought us forth to the life of grace.

---

* John x. 10.　　　　　　　† Is. ix. 6.

On two occasions, then, according to the holy Fathers, Mary became our spiritual Mother.

The first, according to Blessed Albert the Great,* was when she merited to conceive in her virginal womb the Son of God. St. Bernardine of Siena says the same thing more distinctly, for he tells us, "that when at the Annunciation the most blessed Virgin gave the consent which was expected by the Eternal Word before becoming her Son, she from that moment asked our salvation of God with intense ardor, and took it to heart in such a way, that from that moment, as a most loving mother, she bore us in her womb." †

In the second chapter of St. Luke, the Evangelist, speaking of the birth of our blessed Redeemer, says that Mary "brought forth her first-born Son." ‡ Then, remarks an author, "since the Evangelist asserts that on this occasion the most Holy Virgin brought forth her first-born, must we suppose that she had afterwards other children?" But then he replies to his own question, saying, "that as it is of faith that Mary had no other children according to the flesh than Jesus, she must have had other spiritual children, and we are those children." This was revealed by Our Lord to St. Gertrude, § who was one day reading the above text, and was perplexed and could not understand how Mary, being only the Mother of Jesus, could be said to have brought forth her first-born. God explained it to her, saying, that Jesus was Mary's first-born according to the flesh, but that all mankind were her second-born according to the spirit. ‖

---

* *De Laud. B.M.* l. 6, c. 1.
† *Pro Fest. V. M.* s. 8, a. 2, c. 2.　　‡ *Luke* ii. 7.
§ *Spann. Polyanth. litt. m.* t. 6.　　‖ *Insin.* l. 4, c. 3.

From what has been said, we can understand that passage of the sacred Canticles : " Thy belly is like a heap of wheat, set about with lilies," * and which applies to Mary. And it is explained by St. Ambrose, who says : " That although in the most pure womb of Mary there was but one grain of corn, which was Jesus Christ, yet it is called a heap of wheat, because all the elect were virtually contained in it ; " and as Mary was also to be their Mother, in bringing forth Jesus, He was truly and is called the first-born of many brethren.† And the Abbot St. William writes in the same sense, saying, " that Mary, in bringing forth Jesus, our Saviour and our life, brought forth many unto salvation ; and by giving birth to life itself, she gave life to many." ‡

The second occasion on which Mary became our spiritual Mother, and brought us forth to the life of grace, was when she offered to the Eternal Father the life of her beloved Son on Mount Calvary, with so bitter sorrow and suffering. So that St. Augustine declares, that " as she then coöperated by her love in the birth of the faithful to the life of grace, she became the spiritual Mother of all who are members of the one Head, Christ Jesus." § This we are given to understand by the following verse of the sacred Canticles, and which refers to the most blessed Virgin : " They have made me the keeper in the vineyards ; my vineyard I have not kept." ‖ St. William says, that " Mary, in order that she might save many souls, exposed her own to death " ;¶ meaning, that to save us she sacrificed the life of her Son. And who but

---

* Cant. vii. 2. † *Ap. Novar. Umbra V.* c. 63.
‡ *Delrio, in Cant.* iv. 13. § *De S. Virginitate,* c. vi.
‖ Cant. i. 5. ¶ *Delrio, In Cant.* i. 6.

Jesus was the soul of Mary? He was her life, and all her love. And therefore the prophet Simeon foretold that a sword of sorrow would one day transpierce her own most blessed soul.* And it was precisely the lance which transpierced the side of Jesus, Who was the soul of Mary. Then it was that this most blessed Virgin brought us forth by her sorrows to eternal life : and thus we can all call ourselves the children of the sorrows of Mary. Our most loving Mother was always, and in all, united to the will of God. " And therefore," says St. Bonaventure, " when she saw the love of the Eternal Father towards men to be so great that, in order to save them, He willed the death of His Son ; and, on the other hand, seeing the love of the Son in wishing to die for us : in order to conform herself to this excessive love of both the Father and the Son towards the human race, she also with her entire will offered, and consented to, the death of her Son, in order that we might be saved." †

It is true that according to the prophecy of Isaias Jesus, in dying for the redemption of the human race, chose to be alone. " I have trodden the winepress alone " ; ‡ but, seeing the ardent desire of Mary to aid in the salvation of man, He disposed it so that she, by the sacrifice and offering of the life of her Jesus, should cooperate in our salvation, and thus become the Mother of our souls. This Our Saviour signified, when, before expiring, He looked down from the cross on His Mother and on the disciple St. John, who stood at its foot, and, first addressing Mary, He said, " Behold thy son ; " § as it were saying, Behold, the whole human race, which by the offer thou makest of My

---

* Luke ii. 35.   † *In Sent.* l. i. d. 48, a. 2, q. 2.
‡ Is. lxiii. 3.   § John xix. 26.

life for the salvation of all, is even now being born to
the life of grace. Then, turning to the disciple, He
said, " Behold thy Mother." *   " By these words," says
St. Bernardine of Siena, " Mary, by reason of the
love she bore them, became the Mother, not only of
St. John, but of all men." †   And Silveria remarks,
that St. John himself, in stating this fact in his Gospel,
says : " Then He said to the disciple, Behold thy
Mother." Here observe well that Jesus Christ did
not address Himself to John, but to the disciple, in
order to show that He then gave Mary to all who are
His disciples, that is to say, to all Christians, that she
might be their Mother. " John is but the name of
one, whereas the word disciple is applicable to all ;
therefore Our Lord makes use of a name common to
all, to show that Mary was given as a Mother to us."‡

The Church applies to Mary these words of the sacred Canticles : " I am the Mother of fair love" ; § and
a commentator explaining them, says, that the Blessed
Virgin's love renders our souls beautiful in the sight of
God, and also makes her as a most loving mother
receive us as her children, " she being all love towards
those whom she has thus adopted." ‖   And what
mother, exclaims St. Bonaventure, loves her children,
and attends to their welfare, as thou lovest us and
carest for us, O most sweet Queen ! " For dost thou
not love us and seek our welfare far more without
comparison than any earthly mother ?" ¶

Oh, blessed are they who live under the protection of
so loving and powerful a mother ! The prophet David,
although she was not yet born, sought salvation from

---

* John xix. 26.   † *T.I.* s. 51, a. 1, c. 3.
‡ *In Evang.* l. viii. c. 17. q. 14.   § Ecclus. xxiv. 24.
‖ *Paciucch. In* Ps. 86, exc. 22.   ¶ *Stim. div. am.* p. 3, c. 19.

God by dedicating himself as a son of Mary, and thus prayed : " Save the son of Thy handmaid." * Of what handmaid ? " asks St. Augustine; and he answers, " Of her who said, ' Behold the handmaid of the Lord.' " " And who," says Cardinal Bellarmine, "would ever dare to snatch these children from the bosom of Mary, when they have taken refuge there ? What power of hell, or what temptation, can overcome them, if they place their confidence in the patronage of this great Mother, the Mother of God, and of them ? " † There are some who say that when the whale sees its young in danger, either from tempests or pursuers, it opens its mouth and swallows them. This is precisely what Novarinus asserts of Mary: " When the storms of temptation rage, the most compassionate Mother of the faithful with maternal tenderness, protects them as it were in her own bosom until she has brought them into the harbor of salvation."

O most loving Mother ! O most compassionate Mother ! be thou ever blessed; and ever blessed be God, Who has given thee to us for our Mother, and for a secure refuge in all the dangers of this life. Our blessed Lady herself, in a vision, addressed these words to St. Bridget: " As a mother, on seeing her son in the midst of the swords of his enemies, would use every effort to save him, so do I, and will do for all sinners who seek my mercy." ‡ Thus it is that in every engagement with the infernal powers, we shall always certainly conquer by having recourse to the Mother of God, Who is also our Mother, saying and repeating again and again: " We fly to thy patronage, O holy Mother of God : we fly to thy patronage, O holy

---

* Ps. lxxxv. 16.

† *De Sept. Verb.* l. i. c. 12.   ‡ Rev. l. iv. cap. 138.

Mother of God." Oh, how many victories have not
the faithful gained over hell, by having recourse to
Mary with this short but most powerful prayer! Thus
it was that the great servant of God, Sister Mary Crucified, of the Order of St. Benedict, always overcame
the devils.

Be of good heart, then, all you who are children of
Mary. Remember that she accepts as her children all
those who choose to be so. Rejoice! Why do you fear
to be lost, when such a Mother defends and protects
you? "Say, then, O my soul, with great confidence: I
will rejoice and be glad; for whatever the judgment
to be pronounced on me may be, it depends on and
must come from my Brother and Mother." * "Thus,"
says St. Bonaventure, "it is that each one who loves
this good Mother, and relies on her protection, should
animate himself to confidence, remembering that Jesus
is our Brother, and Mary our Mother." The same
thought makes St. Anselm cry out with joy, and encourage us, saying: "O happy confidence! O safe refuge!
the Mother of God is my Mother. How firm, then,
should be our confidence, since our salvation depends
on the judgment of a good Brother and a tender
Mother." † It is, then, our Mother who calls us, and
says, in these words of the Book of Proverbs: "He
that is a little one, let him turn to me." ‡ Children
have always on their lips their mother's name, and in
every fear, in every danger they immediately cry out,
mother! mother! Ah, most sweet Mary! ah, most
loving Mother! this is precisely what thou desirest:
that we should become children, and call on thee in
every danger, and at all times have recourse to thee,

* *Solil.* c. I.   † *Or.* 51.   ‡ Prov. ix. 4.

because thou desirest to help and save us, as thou hast saved all who have had recourse to thee.

Prayer.

O most holy Mother Mary, how is it possible that I, having so holy a mother, should be so wicked? a mother all burning with the love of God, and I loving creatures ; a mother so rich in virtue, and I so poor? Ah, amiable Mother, it is true that I do not deserve any longer to be thy son, for by my wicked life I have rendered myself unworthy of so great an honor. I am satisfied that thou shouldst accept me for thy servant; and in order to be admitted amongst the vilest of them, I am ready to renounce all the kingdoms of the world. Yes, I am satisfied. But still thou must not forbid me to call thee mother. This name consoles and fills me with tenderness, and reminds me of my obligation to love thee. This name excites me to great confidence in thee. When my sins and the divine justice fill me most with consternation, I am all consoled at the thought that thou art my mother. Allow me then to call thee mother, my most amiable mother. Thus do I call thee, and thus will I always call thee. Thou, after God, must be my hope, my refuge, my love in this valley of tears. Thus do I hope to die, breathing forth my soul into thy holy hands, and saying, My Mother, my Mother Mary, help me, have pity on me! Amen.

III. The Greatness of the Love which this Mother bears us.

Since Mary is our Mother, we may consider how great is the love she bears us; love towards our children is a necessary impulse of nature; and St. Thomas[*] says that this is the reason why the divine law imposes

[*] *De Dil. Chr.* c. 13.

on children the obligation of loving their parents; but gives no express command that parents should love their children, for nature itself has so strongly implanted it in all creatures, that, as St. Ambrose remarks, " we know that a mother will expose herself to danger for her children," and even the most savage beasts cannot do otherwise than love their young.* It is said that even tigers, on hearing the cry of their cubs taken by hunters, will go into the sea and swim until they reach the vessel in which they are. Since the very tigers, says our most loving Mother Mary, cannot forget their young, how can I forget to love you, my children? And even, she adds, were such a thing possible as that a mother should forget to love her child, it is not possible that I should cease to love a soul that has become my child: " Can a woman forget her infant, so as not to have pity on the son of her womb? And if she should forget, yet will I not forget thee." †

Mary is our Mother, not, as we have already observed, according to the flesh, but by love; " I am the Mother of fair love; ‡ hence it is the love only that she bears us that makes her our mother; and therefore some one remarks " that she glories in being a mother of love, because she is all love towards us whom she has adopted for her children." § And who can ever tell the love that Mary bears us miserable creatures? Arnold of Chartres tells us that " at the death of Jesus Christ she desired with immense ardor to die with her Son, for love of us;" ‖ so much so,

---

* *Hexam.* 1. 6, c. 4.
† Is. xlix. 15. ‡ Ecclus. xxiv. 24.
§ *Paciucch.* . *In* Ps. 86, Exc. 22. ‖ *Ibid.* Exc. 1.

adds St. Ambrose, that whilst " her Son was hanging on the cross, Mary offered herself to the executioners," * to give her life for us.

But let us consider the reason of this love ; for then we shall be better able to understand how much this good mother loves us.

The first reason for the great love that Mary bears to men, is the great love that she bears to God ; love towards God and love towards our neighbor belong to the same commandment, as expressed by St. John : " this commandment we have from God, that he who loveth God, love also his brother ; " † so that as the one becomes greater the other also increases. What have not the saints done for their neighbor in consequence of their love towards God ! Read only the account of the labors of St. Francis Xavier in the Indies, where, in order to aid the souls of these poor barbarians and bring them to God, he exposed himself to a thousand dangers, clambering amongst the mountains, and seeking out these poor creatures in the caves in which they dwelt like wild beasts. See a St. Francis de Sales, who, in order to convert the heretics of the province of Chablais, risked his life every morning, for a whole year, crawling on his hands and feet over a frozen beam, in order that he might preach to them on the opposite side of a river ; a St. Paulinus, who delivered himself up as a slave, in order that he might obtain liberty for the son of a poor widow ; a St. Fidelis, who, in order to draw the heretics of a certain place to God, persisted in going to preach to them, though he knew it would cost him his life. The saints, then, because they loved God

---

* *Inst. Virg.* c. 7.   † I John iv. 21.

much, did much for their neighbor; but whoever loved God as much as Mary? She loved Him more in the first moment of her existence than all the saints and angels ever loved Him, or will love Him; but this we shall explain at length, when treating of her virtues. Our blessed Lady herself revealed to Sister Mary the Crucified, that the fire of love with which she was inflamed towards God was such that if the heavens and earth were placed in it they would be instantly consumed; so that the ardors of the seraphim, in comparison with it, were but as fresh breezes. And as amongst all the blessed spirits, there is not one that loves God more than Mary, so we neither have nor can have any one who, after God, loves us as much as this most loving Mother; and if we consecrate all the love that mothers bear their children, husbands and wives one another, all the love of angels and saints for their clients, it does not equal the love of Mary towards a single soul. Father Nieremberg * says that the love that all mothers have ever had for their children is but a shadow in comparison with the love that Mary bears to each one of us; and he adds, that she alone loves us more than all the angels and saints put together.

Moreover, our Mother loves us much, because we were recommended to her by her beloved Jesus, when He before expiring said to her, " Woman, behold thy son ! " for we were all represented in the person of St. John, as we have already observed : these were His last words ; and the last recommendations left before death by persons we love are always treasured and never forgotten.

But again, we are exceedingly dear to Mary on ac-

---

* *De Aff. erga B. V.* c. 14.

count of the sufferings we cost her. Mothers generally love those children most, the preservation of
whose life has cost them the most suffering and
anxiety ; we are those children for whom Mary, in
order to obtain for us the life of grace, was obliged to
endure the bitter agony of herself offering her beloved Jesus to die an ignominious death, and had also
to see Him expire before her own eyes in the midst of
the most cruel and unheard-of torments. It was then
by this great offering of Mary that we were bo n to
the life of grace ; we are therefore her very dear children, since we cost her so great suffering. And thus,
as it is written of the love of the Eternal Father
towards men, in giving His own Son to death for us,
that " God so loved the world as to give His only-begotten Son." * " So also," says St. Bonaventure, " we
can say of Mary, that she has so loved us as to give
her only-begotten Son for us." And when did she
give Him ? She gave Him, says Father Nieremberg,
when she granted Him permission to deliver Himself
up to death ; she gave Him to us, when, others neg-
lecting to do so, either out of hatred or from fear, she
might herself have pleaded for the life of her Son before the judges. Well may it be supposed that the
words of so wise and loving a mother would have had
great weight, at least with Pilate, and might have prevented him from sentencing a man to death Whom he
knew and had declared to be innocent. But no, Mary
would not say a word in favor of her Son, lest she
might prevent that death on which our salvation de-
pended. Finally, she gave Him to us a thousand
and a thousand times, during the three hours preced-

* John iii. 16.

ing His death, and which she spent at the foot of the cross ; for during the whole of that time she unceasingly offered, with the extreme of sorrow and the extreme of love, the life of her Son in our behalf, and this with such constancy, that St. Anselm and St. Antoninus say,* that if executioners had been wanting, she herself would have crucified Him, in order to obey the Eternal Father Who willed His death for our salvation. If Abraham had such fortitude as to be ready to sacrifice with his own hands the life of his son, with far greater fortitude would Mary (far more holy and obedient than Abraham) have sacrificed the life of hers. But let us return to the consideration of the gratitude we owe to Mary for so great an act of love as was the painful sacrifice of the life of her Son, which she made to obtain eternal salvation for us all. God abundantly rewarded Abraham for the sacrifice he was prepared to make of his son Isaac ; but we, what return can we make to Mary for the life of her Jesus, a son far more noble and beloved than the son of Abraham? " This love of Mary," says St. Bonaventure, "has indeed obliged us to love her ; for we see that she has surpassed all others in love towards us, since she has given her only Son, Whom she loved more than herself, for us." †

From this arises another motive for the love of Mary towards us; for in us she beholds that which has been purchased at the price of the death of Jesus Christ. If a mother knew that a servant had been ransomed by a beloved son at the price of twenty years of imprisonment and suffering, how greatly would she esteem that servant on this account alone ! Mary well knows that her Son came into the world only

* P. 4, t. 15, c. 41, § 1.   † *De B. V. M.* s. 1.

to save us poor creatures, as He Himself protested, " I am come to save that which is lost." * And to save us He was pleased even to lay down His life for us " Having become obedient unto death." † If, then, Mary loved us but little, she would show that she valued but little the blood of her Son, which was the price of our salvation. To St. Elizabeth of Hungary it was revealed that Mary, from the time she dwelt in the Temple, did nothing but pray for us, begging that God would hasten the coming of His Son into the world to save us. And how much more must we suppose that she loves us, now that she has seen that we are valued to such a degree by her Son, that He did not disdain to purchase us at such a cost.

Because all men have been redeemed by Jesus, therefore Mary loves and protects them all. It was she who was seen by St. John in the Apocalypse, clothed with the sun : " And a great sign appeared in heaven : a woman clothed with the sun." ‡ She is said to be clothed with the sun, because as there is no one on earth who can be hidden from the heat of the sun—" There is no one that can hide himself from His heat" §—so there is no one living who can be deprived of the love of Mary. " From its heat," that is, as blessed Raymond Jordano applies the words, " from the love of Mary." ‖ " And who," exclaims St. Antoninus, " can ever form an idea of the tender care that this most loving Mother takes of all of us," " offering and dispensing her mercy to every one : "¶ for our good Mother desired the salvation of all, and cooperated in obtaining it. " It is evident," says St.

* Luke xix. 10.   † Phil. ii. 8.
‡ Apoc. xii. 1.   § Ps. xviii. 7.
‖ *Contempl. de V. M. in prol.*
¶ P. 4, t. 15, c. 2.

Bernard, "that she was solicitous for the whole human race."* Hence the custom of some of Mary's clients, spoken of by Cornelius à Lapide, and which consists in asking Our Lord to grant them the graces that our blessed Lady seeks for them, succeeds most advantageously. They say, Lord, grant me that which the most blessed Virgin Mary asks for me. "And no wonder," adds the same writer, "for our Mother desires for us better things than we can possibly desire ourselves." The devout Bernardine de Bustis says, that Mary "loves to do us good, and dispense graces to us far more than we to receive them." †
On this subject Blessed Albert the Great applies to Mary the words of the Book of Wisdom : "She preventeth them that covet her, so that she first showeth herself unto them." ‡ Mary anticipates those who have recourse to her by making them find her before they seek her. "The love that this good Mother bears us is so great," says Richard of St. Laurence, "that as soon as she perceives our want she comes to our assistance. She comes before she is called." §

And now, if Mary is so good to all, even to the ungrateful and negligent, who love her but little, and seldom have recourse to her, how much more loving will she be to those who love her and often call upon her ! "She is easily found by them that seek her." ‖ "Oh, how easy," adds the same Blessed Albert, "is it for those who love Mary to find her, and to find her full of compassion and love ! " In the words of the Book of Proverbs, "I love them that love me," ¶ she protests that she cannot do otherwise than love those who love her. And although this most loving Lady

---

* *In Assumpt.* s. 4. † *Marial*, p. 2, s. 5.
‡ Wis. vi. 14. § *In Cant.* c. 23.
‖ Wis. vi. 13. ¶ Prov. viii. 17,

loves all men as her children, yet, says St. Bernard, "she recognizes and loves," * that is, she loves in a more special manner, those who love her more tenderly.   Blessed Raymond Jordano asserts that these happy lovers of Mary are not only loved but even served by her ; for he says that those who find the most blessed Virgin Mary, find all ; for she loves those who love her, nay more, she serves those who serve her. †

In the chronicles of the Order of St. Dominic it is related that one of the friars, named Leonard, used to recommend himself two hundred times a day.to this Mother of Mercy, and that when he was attacked by his last illness he saw a most beautiful queen by his side, who thus addressed him: "Leonard, wilt thou die, and come and dwell with my Son and with me?" "And who art thou?" he replied. "I am," said the most blessed Virgin, for she it was, "I am the Mother of Mercy: thou hast so many times invoked me, behold, I am now come to take thee; let us go together to paradise." On the same day Leonard died, and, as we trust, followed her to the kingdom of the blessed.

"Ah, most sweet Mary!" exclaimed the Venerable John Berchmans, of the Society of Jesus, "blessed is he who loves thee! If I love Mary, I am certain of perseverance, and shall obtain whatever I wish from God." Therefore the devout youth was never tired of renewing his resolution, and of repeating often to himself : "I will love Mary; I will love Mary."

Oh, how much does the love of this good Mother exceed that of all her children! Let them love her

---

* *In Salve Reg.* s. I.   † *Contempl. de V. M. in prol,*

as much as they will, Mary is always amongst lovers
the most loving, says St. Ignatius the martyr.

Let them love her as did St. Stanislas Kostka,
who loved this dear Mother so tenderly, that in speaking of her he moved all who heard him to love her.
He had made new words and new titles with which
to honor her name. He never did anything without
first turning to her image to ask her blessing. When
he said her office, the Rosary, or other prayers, he did
so with the same external marks of affection as he
would have done had he been speaking face to face
with Mary; when the *Salve Regina* was sung, his
whole soul, and even his whole countenance, was all
inflamed with love. On being one day asked by a
Father of the Society, who was going with him to visit
a picture of the Blessed Virgin, how much he loved
Mary,—" Father," he answered, " what more can I
say? she is my mother." " But," adds the Father,
" the holy youth uttered these words with such tenderness in his voice, with such an expression of countenance, and at the same time it came so fully from
his heart, that it no longer seemed to be a young man,
but rather an angel speaking of the love of Mary."

Let us love her as Blessed Hermann loved her.
He called her the spouse of his love, for he was
honored by Mary herself with this same title. Let us
love her as did St. Philip Neri, who was filled with
consolation at the mere thought of Mary, and therefore called her his delight. Let us love her as did St.
Bonaventure, who called her not only his Lady and
Mother, but to show the tenderness of his affection,
even called her his heart and soul : " Hail, my Lady,
my Mother; nay, even my heart, my soul ! "

Let us love her like that great lover of Mary, St. Bernard, who loved this his sweet Mother so much that he called her the ravisher of hearts ; * and to express the ardent love he bore her, added : "for hast thou not ravished my heart, O Queen ? " †

Let us call her beloved, like St. Bernardine of Siena, who daily went to visit a devotional picture of Mary, and there, in tender colloquies with his Queen, declared his love ; and when asked where he went each day he replied that he went to visit his beloved.

Let us love her as did St. Aloysius Gonzaga, whose love for Mary burnt so unceasingly, that whenever he heard the sweet name of his Mother mentioned his heart was instantly inflamed, and his countenance lighted up with a fire that was visible to all.

Let us love her as much as St. Francis Solano did, who, maddened as it were (but with a holy madness) with love for Mary, would sing before her picture, and accompany himself on a musical instrument, saying, that, like worldly lovers, he serenaded his most sweet Queen.

Finally, let us love her as so many of her servants have loved her, who never could do enough to show their love. Father John of Trexo, of the Society of Jesus, rejoiced in the name of slave of Mary; and as a mark of servitude, went often to visit her in some church dedicated in her honor. On reaching the church he poured out abundant tears of tenderness and love for Mary; then, prostrating, he licked and rubbed the pavement with his tongue and face, kissing it a thousand times, because it was the house of his beloved Lady. Father James Martinez, of the same Society, who for his devotion for our blessed

* *Ib.* † *Med. in Salve Reg.*

Lady on her feasts was carried by angels to heaven
to see how they were kept there, used to say, " Would
that I had the hearts of all angels and saints, to love
Mary as they love her—would that I had the lives of
all men, to give them all for her love ! "

Oh, that others would come to love her as did
Charles, the son of St. Bridget, who said that nothing
in the world consoled him so much as the knowledge
that Mary was so greatly loved by God. And he
added, that he would willingly endure every torment
rather than allow Mary to lose the smallest degree of
her glory, were such a thing possible; and that if her
glory was his, he would renounce it in her favor, as
being far more worthy of it.

Let us, moreover, desire to lay down our lives as a
testimony of our love for Mary, as Alphonsus Rodriguez desired to do. Let us love her as did those who
even cut the beloved name of Mary on their breasts
with sharp instruments, as did Francis Binanzio and
Radagundis, wife of King Clothaire, or as did those
who could imprint this loved name on their flesh with
hot irons, in order that it might remain more distinct
and lasting; as did her devout servants Baptist Ar-
chinto and Augustine d'Espinosa, both of the Society
of Jesus, impelled thereto by the vehemence of their
love.

Let us, in fine, do or desire to do all that it is possible for a lover to do, who intends to make his affection
known to the person loved. For be assured that the
lovers of Mary will never be able to equal her in
love. " I know, O Lady," says St. Peter Damian, " that
thou art most loving, and that thou lovest us with an
invincible love." * I know, my Lady, that among

* *In Nat. B. V.* s. I.

those that love thee thou lovest the most, and that
thou lovest us with a love that can never be surpassed.

The blessed Alphonsus Rodriguez, of the Society of
Jesus, once prostrate before an image of Mary, felt his
heart inflamed with love towards this most holy Virgin, and burst forth into the following exclamation:
"My most beloved Mother, I know that thou lovest
me, but thou dost not love me as much as I love thee."
Mary, as it were offended on the point of love, immediately replied from the image : "What dost thou
say, Alphonsus—what dost thou say ? Oh, how much
greater is the love that I bear thee than any love that
thou canst have for me! Know that the distance
between heaven and earth is not so great as the distance between thy love and mine."

St. Bonaventure, then, was right in exclaiming:
Blessed are they who have the good fortune to be
faithful servants and lovers of this most loving Mother.
"Blessed are the hearts of those who love Mary;
blessed are they who are tenderly devoted to her." *
Yes ; for "in this struggle our most gracious Queen
never allows her clients to conquer her in love. She
returns our love and homage, and always increases her
past favors by new ones." † Mary, imitating in this
our most loving Redeemer Jesus Christ, returns to
those who love her their love doubled in benefits and
favors.

Then will I exclaim, with the enamoured St. Anselm, "May my heart languish and my soul melt and be
consumed with your love, O my beloved Saviour Jesus,
and my dear Mother Mary! But, as without your

---

* *Psalt. B. V. ps.* xxxi., cxviii.
† *Paciucch. in* Ps. lxxxvi. *Exc.* 2.

grace I cannot love you, grant me, O Jesus and Mary, grant my soul, by your merits and not mine, the grace to love you as you deserve to be loved. O God, lover of men, Thou couldst love guilty men even unto death. And canst Thou deny Thy love and that of Thy Mother to those who ask it?" *

Prayer.

O Lady, O ravisher of hearts! I will exclaim with St. Bonaventure: " Lady, who with the love and favor thou showest thy servants dost ravish their hearts, ravish also my miserable heart, which desires ardently to love thee. Thou, my Mother, hast enamoured a God with thy beauty, and drawn Him from heaven into thy chaste womb; and shall I live without loving thee? " No, I will say to thee with one of thy most loving sons, John Berchmans of the Society of Jesus, I will never rest until I am certain of having obtained thy love; but a constant and tender love towards thee, my Mother, who hast loved me with so much tenderness," even when I was ungrateful towards thee. And what should I now be, O Mary, if thou hadst not obtained so many mercies for me? Since, then, thou didst love me so much when I loved thee not, how much more may I not now hope from thee, now that I love thee? I love thee, O my Mother, and I would that I had a heart to love thee in place of all those unfortunate creatures who love thee not. I would that I could speak with a thousand tongues, that all might know thy greatness, thy holiness, thy mercy, and the love with which thou lovest all who love thee. Had I riches, I would employ them all for thy honor. Had I subjects, I would make them all thy lovers. In fine, if the occasion presented itself I would lay down my life for thy glory. I love thee, then, O my Mother; but at the same time I fear that I do not love thee as I ought; for I hear that love makes lovers

* *Orat.* 51.

like the person loved. If, then, I see myself so unlike thee, it is a mark that I do not love thee. Thou art so pure, and I defiled with many sins ; thou so humble, and I so proud ; thou so holy, and I so wicked. This, then, is what thou hast to do, O Mary ; since thou lovest me, make me like thee. Thou hast all power to change hearts ; take, then, mine, and change it. Show the world what thou canst do for those who love thee. Make me a saint ; make me thy worthy child. This is my hope.

IV. Mary is the Mother of Penitent Sinners.

Our blessed Lady told St. Bridget that she was the mother not only of the just and innocent, but also of sinners, provided they were willing to repent.* Oh, how prompt does a sinner (desirous of amendment, and who flies to her feet) find this good Mother to embrace and help him, far more so than any earthly mother ! St. Gregory VII. wrote in this sense to the princess Matilda, saying : " Resolve to sin no more, and I promise that undoubtedly thou wilt find Mary more ready to love thee than any earthly mother." †

But whoever aspires to be a child of this great mother, must first abandon sin, and then may hope to be accepted as such. Richard of St. Laurence, on the words of Proverbs, " up rose her children," ‡ remarks that the words " up rose " come first, and then the word " children," to show that no one can be a child of Mary without first endeavoring to rise from the fault into which he has fallen ; for he who is in mortal sin is not worthy to be called the son of such a mother. § And St. Peter Chrysologus says that he who acts in a different manner from Mary declares

---

* Rev. l. iv. c. 138.   † *Lib.* i. ep. 47.
‡ Prov. xxxi. 28.   § *De Laud. B. V.* lib. ii. p. 5.

thereby that he will not be her son. " He who does
not the works of his mother, abjures his lineage." *
Mary humble, and he proud ; Mary pure, and he
wicked ; Mary full of love, and he hating his neighbor. He gives thereby proof that he is not, and will
not be, the son of his holy Mother. The sons of
Mary, says Richard of St. Laurence, are her imitators,
and this chiefly in three things : in " chastity, liberality, and humility ; and also in meekness, mercy, and
such like." †

Whilst disgusting her by a wicked life, who would
dare even to wish to be the child of Mary ? A certain
sinner once said to Mary, " Show thyself a Mother ;"
but the Blessed Virgin replied, " Show thyself a son." ‡
Another invoked the divine Mother, calling her the
Mother of mercy, and she answered : " You sinners
when you want my help call me Mother of Mercy, and
at the same time do not cease by your sins to make
me a Mother of sorrows and anguish." § " He is
cursed of God," says Ecclesiasticus, " that angereth
his mother." ‖ " That is Mary," ¶ says Richard of St.
Laurence. God curses those who by their wicked life,
and still more by their obstinacy in sin, afflict this
tender Mother.

I say, by their obstinacy; for if a sinner, though he
may not as yet have given up his sin, endeavors to do
so, and for this purpose seeks the help of Mary, this
good Mother will not fail to assist him, and make him
recover the grace of God. And this is precisely what
St. Bridget heard one day from the lips of Jesus

---

* *Serm.* 123.   † *Loco cit.*
‡ *Auriem, Aff. Scamb.* p. 3, c. 12.
§ *Pelb. Stell.* l. xii. p. ult. c. 7.   ‖ Ecclus. iii. 18.
¶ *De Laud. B. M.* l. 2, p. 1.

Christ, Who, speaking to His Mother, said, " Thou assistest him who endeavors to return to God, and thy consolations are never wanting to any one."*   So long, then, as a sinner is obstinate, Mary cannot love him; but if he (finding himself chained by some passion which keeps him a slave of hell) recommends himself to the Blessed Virgin, and implores her, with confidence and perseverance, to withdraw him from the state of sin in which he is, there can be no doubt but this good Mother will extend her powerful hand to him, will deliver him from his chains, and lead him to a state of salvation.

The doctrine that all prayers and works performed in a state of sin are sins was condemned as heretical by the sacred Council of Trent.†   St. Bernard says,‡ that although prayer in the mouth of a sinner is devoid of beauty, as it is unaccompanied with charity, nevertheless it is useful, and obtains grace to abandon sin; for, as St. Thomas teaches,§ the prayer of a sinner, though without merit, is an act which obtains the grace of forgiveness, since the power of impetration is founded not on the merits of him who asks, but on the divine goodness, and the merits and promises of Jesus Christ, Who has said, " Every one that asketh receiveth." ‖   The same thing must be said of prayers offered to the divine Mother.   " If he who prays," says St. Anselm, "does not merit to be heard, the merits of the Mother, to whom he recommends himself, will intercede effectually." ¶

Therefore, St. Bernard exhorts all sinners to have recourse to Mary, invoking her with great confidence;

---

* *Rev.* l. 4, c. 19.   † *Sess.* vi. *can.* 7.
‡ *De Div.* s. 81.   §2. 2, q. 178, a. 2.
‖ Luke xi. 10.   ¶ *De Excell. Virg.* c. 6.

for though the sinner does not himself merit the graces which he asks, yet he receives them, because the Blessed Virgin asks and obtains them from God, on account of her own merits. These are His words, addressing a sinner: " Because thou wast unworthy to receive the grace thyself, it was given to Mary, in order that, through her, thou mightest receive all." *
" If a mother," continues the same saint, " knew that her two sons bore a mortal enmity to each other, and that each plotted against the other's life, would she not exert herself to her utmost in order to reconcile them ? This would be the duty of a good mother. And thus it is," the saint goes on to say, " that Mary acts; for she is the Mother of Jesus, and the Mother of men. When she sees a sinner at enmity with Jesus Christ, she cannot endure it, and does all in her power to make peace between them. O happy Mary, thou art the Mother of the criminal, and the Mother of the judge; and being the Mother of both, they are thy children, and thou canst not endure discords amongst them." †

This most benign Lady only requires that the sinner should recommend himself to her, and purpose amendment. When Mary sees a sinner at her feet, imploring her mercy, she does not consider the crimes with which he is loaded, but the intention with which he comes; and if this is good, even should he have committed all possible sins, the most loving Mother embraces him, and does not disdain to heal the wounds of his soul; for she is not only called the Mother of Mercy, but is so truly and indeed, and shows herself such by the love and tenderness with which she assists

* *In Vig. Nat.* s. 3.
† *Ap. S. Bonav. Spec. B. V. lect.* 3.

us all. And this is precisely what the Blessed Virgin herself said to St. Bridget: "However much a man sins, I am ready immediately to receive him when he repents; nor do I pay attention to the number of his sins, but only to the intention with which he comes. I do not disdain to anoint and heal his wounds; for I am called, and truly am, the Mother of Mercy." *

Mary is the Mother of sinners who wish to repent, and as a mother she cannot do otherwise than compassionate them; nay more, she seems to feel, the miseries of her poor children as if they were her own. When the Canaanitish woman begged Our Lord to deliver her daughter from the devil who possessed her, she said, "Have mercy on me, O Lord, Thou Son of David, my daughter is grievously troubled by a devil." †But since the daughter, and not the mother, was tormented, she should rather have said, "Lord, take compassion on my daughter:" and not, Have mercy on me; but no, she said, "Have mercy on me," and she was right; for the sufferings of children are felt by their mother as if they were their own. And it is precisely thus, says Richard of St. Laurence, that Mary prays to God when she recommends a sinner to Him who has had recourse to her ; she cries out for the sinful soul. "Have mercy on *me !*" "My Lord," she seems to say, "this poor soul that is in sin is my daughter, and therefore, pity not so much her as me, who am her mother." ‡

Would that all sinners had recourse to this sweet Mother ! for then certainly all would be pardoned by God. "O Mary," exclaims St. Bonaventure, in rapturous astonishment, "thou embracest with maternal

---

* Rev. 1. 2, c. 23.—1. 6, c. 117.
† Matt. xv. 22.   ‡ *De Laud. B. M.* 1. 6.

affections a sinner despised by the whole world, nor dost thou leave him until thou hast reconciled the poor creature with his Judge ; " meaning that the sinner, whilst in the state of sin, is hated and loathed by all, even by inanimate creatures ; fire, air, and earth would chastise him, and avenge the honor of their outraged Lord. But if this unhappy creature flies to Mary, will Mary reject him? Oh, no : provided he goes to her for help, and in order to amend, she will embrace him with the affection of a mother, and will not let him go, until, by her powerful intercession, she has reconciled him with God, and reinstated him in grace.

In the Second Book of Kings, we read that a wise woman of Thecua addressed King David in the following words : " My lord, I had two sons, and for my misfortune, one killed the other ; so that I have now lost one, and justice demands the other, the only one that is left; take compassion on a poor mother, and let me not be thus deprived of both." David, moved with compassion toward the mother, declared that the delinquent should be set at liberty and restored to her. Mary seems to say the same thing when God is indignant against a sinner who has recommended himself to her. " My God," she says, " I had two sons, Jesus and man ; man took the life of my Jesus on the cross, and now Thy justice would condemn the guilty one. O Lord, my Jesus is already dead, have pity on me, and if I have lost the one, do not make me lose the other also."

Most certainly God will not condemn those sinners who have recourse to Mary, and for whom she prays, since He Himself commended them to her as her children. The devout Lanspergius supposes Our Lord speaking in the following terms : " I recommended all, but especially sinners, to Mary, as her children, and therefore is she so diligent and so careful in the exercise of her office, that she allows none of those committed to her charge, and especially those who invoke her, to perish ; but as far as she can, brings all to Me." "And who can ever tell," says the devout Blosius, "the goodness, the mercy, the compassion, the love, the benignity, the clemency, the fidelity, the benevolence, the charity, of this virgin Mother towards men ? It is such that no words can express it."

"Let us, then," says St. Bernard, "cast ourselves at the feet of this good mother, and embracing them, let us not depart until she blesses us, and thus accepts us for her children."   And who can ever doubt the compassion of this Mother ? St. Bonaventure used to say : "Even should she take my life, I would still hope in her; and, full of confidence, would desire to die before her image, and be certain of salvation." And thus should each sinner address her when he has recourse to this compassionate Mother ; he should say:

"My Lady and Mother, on account of my sins I deserve that thou shouldst reject me, and even that thou shouldst thyself chastise me according to my deserts ; but shouldst thou reject me, or even take my life, I will still trust in thee, and hope with a firm hope that thou wilt save me.   In thee is all my confidence; only grant me the consolation of dying before thy picture, recommending myself to thy mercy, then I am convinced that I shall not be lost, but that I shall go and praise thee in heaven, in company with so many of thy servants who left this world calling on thee for help, and have all been saved by thy powerful intercession."

Prayer

O my sovereign Queen and worthy Mother of my God, most holy Mary; I seeing myself, as I do, so despicable and loaded with so many sins, ought not to presume to call thee Mother, or even to approach thee; yet I will not allow my miseries to deprive me of the consolation and confidence that I feel in calling thee Mother; I know well that I deserve that thou shouldst reject me; but I beseech thee to remember all that thy Son Jesus has endured for me, and then reject me if thou canst. I am a wretched sinner, who, more than all others, have despised the infinite majesty of God: but the evil is done. To thee have I recourse; thou canst help me; my Mother, help me. Say not that thou canst not do so; for I know that thou art all-powerful, and that thou obtainest whatever thou desirest of God; and if thou sayest that thou wilt not help me, tell me at least to whom I can apply in this my so great misfortune. "Either pity me," will I say with the devout St. Anselm, "O my Jesus, and forgive me, and do thou pity me, my Mother Mary, by interceding for me, or at least tell me to whom I can have recourse, who is more compassionate, or in whom I can have greater confidence than in thee." Oh, no; neither on earth nor in heaven can I find any one who has more compassion for the miserable, or who is better able to assist me, than thou canst, O Mary. Thou, O Jesus, art my Father, and thou, Mary, art my Mother. You both love the most miserable, and go seeking them in order to save them. I deserve hell, and am the most miserable of all. But you need not seek me, nor do I presume to ask so much. I now present myself before you with a certain hope that I shall not be abandoned. Behold me at your feet; my Jesus, forgive me; my Mother Mary, help me.

MARY, MOTHER OF MERCY

CHAPTER II.

Vita, Dulcedo.

OUR LIFE, OUR SWEETNESS.

MARY, OUR LIFE, OUR SWEETNESS.

I. Mary is our Life, because she Obtains for us the Pardon of our Sins.

To understand why the holy Church makes us call Mary our life we must know, that as the soul gives life to the body so does divine grace give life to the soul; for a soul without grace has the name of being alive, but is in truth dead, as it was said of one in the Apocalypse, "Thou hast the name of being alive, and thou art dead."* Mary, then, in obtaining this grace for sinners by her intercession, thus restores them to life.

See how the Church makes her speak, applying to her the following words of Proverbs: "They that in the morning early watch for me shall find me."† They who are diligent in having recourse to me in the morning, that is, as soon as they can, will most certainly find me. In the Septuagint the words "shall find me" are rendered "shall find grace." So that to have recourse to Mary is the same thing as to find the grace of God. A little further on she says, "He that shall find me shall find life, and shall have salvation

---

*Apoc. iii. 1.   † Prov. viii. 17.

from the Lord." "Listen," exclaims St. Bonaventure
on these words, "listen, all you who desire the kingdom of God; honor the most blessed Virgin Mary
and you will find life and eternal salvation."*

St. Bernardine of Siena says, that if God did not
destroy man after his first sin, it was on account of
His singular love for this holy Virgin, who was des-
tined to be born of this race. And the saint adds,
"that he has no doubt but that all the mercies granted
by God under the Old Dispensation were granted only
in consideration of this most blessed Lady."†

Hence St. Bernard was right in exhorting us "to
seek for grace, and to seek it by Mary"; ‡ meaning,
that if we have had the misfortune to lose the grace of
God, we should seek to recover it, but we should do
so through Mary; for though we may have lost it, she
has found it; and hence the saint calls her "the finder
of grace." § The angel Gabriel expressly declared this
for our consolation, when he saluted the Blessed Virgin saying "Fear not, Mary, thou hast found grace." ‖
But if Mary had never been deprived of grace, how
could the archangel say that she had then found it?
A thing may be found by a person who did not pre-
viously possess it; but we are told by the same archangel that the Blessed Virgin was always with God,
always in grace, nay, full of grace. "Hail, full of
grace, the Lord is with thee." Since Mary, then, did
not find grace for herself, she being always full of it,
for whom did she find it? Cardinal Hugo, in his commentary on the above text, replies that she found it for
sinners who had lost it. "Let sinners, then," says this
devout writer, "who by their crimes have lost grace,

* *Psalt. B. V. ps.* 48.   † *Pro Fest. V. M.* s. 5, c. 2.
‡ *De Aquæd.*   § *In. Adv. D.* s. 2.   ‖ Luke i. 30.

address themselves to the Blessed Virgin, for with her
they will surely find it; let them humbly salute her, and
say with confidence, " Lady, that which has been found
must be restored to him who has lost it; restore us,
therefore, our property which thou hast found." On
this subject, Richard of St. Laurence concludes, " that
if we hope to receive the grace of God, we must go to
Mary, who has found it, and finds it always." * And
as she always was and always will be dear to God, if
we have recourse to her we shall certainly succeed.

Again, Mary says, in the eighth chapter of the sacred
Canticles, that God has placed her in the world to be
our defence: " I am a wall: and my breasts are as a
tower." † And she is truly made a mediatress of peace
between sinners and God; " Since I am become in His
presence as one finding peace." On these words St.
Bernard encourages sinners, saying, " Go to this
Mother of Mercy, and show her the wounds which thy
sins have left on thy soul; then will she certainly
entreat her Son, by the breasts that gave Him suck, to
pardon thee all. And this divine Son, Who loves her
so tenderly, will most certainly grant her petition." In
this sense it is that the holy Church, in her almost
daily prayer, calls upon us to beg Our Lord to grant
us the powerful help of the intercession of Mary to
rise from our sins: " Grant Thy help to our weakness,
O most merciful God; and that we who are mindful
of the holy Mother of God, may by the help of her
intercession rise from our iniquities."

With reason, then, does St. Laurence Justinian call
her " the hope of malefactors," ‡ since she alone is
the one who obtains them pardon from God. With

---

* *De Laud. V.* i. 2, p. 5.   † Cant. viii. 10.
‡ *S. de Nat. V. M.*

reason does St. Bernard call her "the sinners' ladder," * since she, the most compassionate Queen, extending her hand to them, draws them from an abyss of sin, and enables them to ascend to God. With reason does an ancient writer call her "the only hope of sinners," for by her help alone can we hope for the remission of our sins. †

St. John Chrysostom also says "that sinners receive pardon by the intercession of Mary alone." And therefore the saint, in the name of all sinners, thus addresses her : "Hail, Mother of God and of us.all, 'heaven,' where God dwells, 'throne,' from which our Lord dispenses all grace, 'fair daughter, Virgin, honor, glory, and firmament of our Church,' assiduously pray to Jesus that in the day of judgment we may find mercy through thee, and receive the reward prepared by God for those who love Him." ‡

With reason, finally, is Mary called, in the words of the sacred Canticles, the dawn : "Who is she that cometh forth as the morning rising ?"§   Yes, says Pope Innocent III., "for as the dawn is the end of night, and the beginning of day, well may the Blessed Virgin Mary, who was the end of vices, be called the dawn of day." ‖   When devotion towards Mary begins in a soul it produces the same effect that the birth of this most holy Virgin produced in the world. It puts an end to the night of sin, and leads the soul into the path of virtue. Therefore, St. Germanus says, "O Mother of God, thy protection never ceases, thy intercession is life, and thy patronage never fails." ¶   And in a sermon the same saint says, that to pronounce the name

* *De Aquæd.* † *Serm.* 194, *E. B. app.*
‡ *Off. B. M. lect.* 6. § Cant. vi. 9.
‖ *In Assumpt.* s. 2. ¶ *In Dorm. B. V.* s. 2.

of Mary with affection is a sign of life in the soul, or
at least that life will soon return there.

We read in the Gospel of St Luke that Mary said,
" Behold, from henceforth all generations shall call
me blessed." *　" Yes, my Lady," exclaims St. Bernard, " all generations shall call thee blessed, for thou
hast begotten life and glory for all generations of
men." †　For this cause all men shall call thee blessed,
for all thy servants obtain through thee the life of
grace and eternal glory.　" In thee do sinners find
pardon, and the just perseverance and eternal life." ‡
" Distrust not, O sinner," says the devout Bernardine
de Bustis, " even if thou hast committed all possible
sins : go with confidence to this most glorious Lady,
and thou wilt find her hands filled with mercy and
bounty."　And, he adds, for " she desires more to do
thee good than thou canst desire to receive favors
from her." §

St. Andrew of Crete calls Mary the pledge of divine
mercy ; ‖ meaning that, when sinners have recourse to
Mary, that they may be reconciled with God, He as-
sures them of pardon and gives them a pledge of it ;
and this pledge is Mary, whom He has bestowed upon
us for our advocate, and by whose intercession (by
virtue of the merits of Jesus Christ) God forgives all
who have recourse to her.　St. Bridget heard an angel
say, that the holy prophets rejoiced in knowing that
God, by the humility and purity of Mary, was to be
reconciled with sinners, and to receive those who had
offended Him to favor.　" They exulted, foreknowing
that Our Lord Himself would be appeased by thy
humility, and the purity of thy life, O Mary, thou

* Luke i. 48.　　† *In Pentec.*　　‡ *In Pentec.* s. 2.
§ *Marial.* p. 2, s. 5.　　‖ *In Dorm. B. V.* s. 3.

supereffulgent star, and that He would be reconciled with those who had provoked His wrath." *

No sinner having recourse to the compassion of Mary should fear being rejected ; for she is the Mother of Mercy, and as such desires to save the most miserable. Mary is that happy ark, says St. Bernard, " in which those who take refuge will never suffer the shipwreck of eternal perdition." † At the time of the deluge even brutes were saved in Noe's ark. Under the mantle of Mary even sinners obtain salvation. St. Gertrude once saw Mary with her mantle extended, and under it many wild beasts—lions, bears, and tigers —had taken refuge.‡ And she remarked that Mary not only did not reject, but even welcomed and caressed, them with the greatest tenderness. The saint understood hereby that the most abandoned sinners who have recourse to Mary are not only not rejected, but that they are welcomed and saved by her from eternal death. Let us, then, enter this ark, let us take refuge under the mantle of Mary, and she most certainly will not reject us, but will secure our salvation.

Prayer.

Behold, O Mother of my God, my only hope, Mary, be-hold at thy feet a miserable sinner, who asks thee for mercy. Thou art proclaimed and called by the whole Church, and by all the faithful, the refuge of sinners. Thou art consequently my refuge ; thou hast to save me. I will say with William of Paris : Thou knowest, most sweet Mother of God, how much thy blessed Son desires our salvation.§ Thou knowest all that Jesus Christ en-dured for this end. I present thee, O my Mother, the

---

* *Serm. Ang.* c. 9.   † *S. de B. V. M. Deip.*
‡ *Insin.* l. 4, c. 50.   § *Rhet. Div.* c. 18.

sufferings of Jesus: the cold that He endured in the stable, His journey into Egypt, His toils, His sweat, the blood that He shed ; the anguish which caused His death on the cross, and of which thou wast thyself a witness. Oh, show that thou lovest thy beloved Son, and by this love I implore thee to assist me. Extend thy hand to a poor creature who has fallen and asks thy help. Were I a saint I would not need seek thy mercy ; but because I am a sinner I fly to thee, who art the Mother of mercies. I know that thy compassionate heart finds its consolation in assisting the miserable, when thou canst do so, and dost not find them obstinate. Console, then, thy compassionate heart, and console me this day; for now thou hast the opportunity of saving a poor creature condemned to hell ; and thou canst do so, for I will not be obstinate. I abandon myself into thy hands, only tell me what thou wouldst have me do, and obtain for me strength to execute it, for I am resolved to do all that depends on me to recover the divine grace. I take refuge under thy mantle. Jesus wills that I should have recourse to thee, in order not only that His blood may save me, but also that thy prayers may assist me in this great work ; for thy glory, and for His own, since thou art His Mother. He sends me to thee, that thou mayst help me. O Mary, see, I have recourse to thee; in thee do I confide. Thou prayest for so many others, pray also for me ; say only a word. Tell Our Lord that thou willest my salvation, and God will certainly save me. Say that I am thine, and then I have obtained all that I ask, all that I desire.

II. Mary is also our Life, because she Obtains for us Perseverance.

Final perseverance is so great a gift of God, that (as it was declared by the holy Council of Trent) it is quite gratuitous on His part, and we cannot *merit* it. Yet we are told by St. Augustine, that all who seek for it obtain it from God; and, according to Father Suarez, they obtain it infallibly, if only they are diligent in asking for it to the end of their lives. For, as Bellarmine well remarks, " that which is daily required must be asked for every day." Now, if it is true (and I hold it as certain, according to the now generally received opinion) —— that all the graces that God dispenses to men pass through the hands of Mary, it will be equally true that it is only through Mary that we can hope for this greatest of all graces —perseverance. And we shall obtain it most certainly if we always seek it with confidence through Mary. This grace she herself promises to all who serve her faithfully during life, in the following words of Ecclesiasticus, and which are applied to her by the Church,* on the feast of her Immaculate Conception: " They that work by me shall not sin. They that explain me shall have life everlasting." †

In order that we may be preserved in the life of grace, we require spiritual fortitude to resist the many enemies of our salvation. Now this fortitude can be obtained only by the means of Mary, and we are assured of it in the Book of Proverbs, for the Church applies the passage to this most blessed Virgin.

---

* *Off. Imm. Conc.* † Ecclus. xxiv. 30.

"Strength is mine; by me kings reign;"* meaning
by the words "strength is mine" that God has bestowed this precious gift on Mary, in order that she
may dispense it to her faithful clients. And by the
words "by me kings reign" she signifies that by her
means her servants reign over and command their
senses and passions, and thus become worthy to reign
eternally in heaven. Oh, what strength do the servants of this great Lady possess to overcome all the
assaults of hell! Mary is that tower spoken of in the
sacred Canticles: "Thy neck is as the tower of David,
which is built with bulwarks; a thousand bucklers
hang upon it, all the armor of valiant men."† She
is as a well-defended fortress in defence of her lovers,
who in their wars have recourse to her. In her do
her clients find all shields and arms to defend themselves against hell.

And for the same reason the most blessed Virgin is
called a plane-tree in the words of Ecclesiasticus:
"As a plane-tree by the water in the streets was I exalted."‡ Cardinal Hugo explains them, and says that
the "plane-tree has leaves like shields," to show how
Mary defends all who take refuge with her. Blessed
Amedeus gives another explanation, and says that this
holy Virgin is called a plane-tree because, as the plane
shelters travellers under its branches from the heat of
the sun and from the rain, so do men find refuge
under the mantle of Mary from the ardor of their
passions and from the fury of temptations.§ Truly
are those souls to be pitied who abandon this defence,
in ceasing their devotion to Mary, and no longer
recommending themselves to her in the time of dan-

---

* Prov. viii. 14.—*Off. B. V.*   † Cant. iv. 4.
‡ Ecclus. xxiv. 19.   § *De Laud. B. V. hom.* 8.

ger.   If the sun ceased to rise, says St. Bernard, how could the world become other than a chaos of darkness and horror?   And applying this question to Mary, he repeats it.   " Take away the sun, and where will be the day?   Take away Mary, and what will be left but the darkest night?" *   When a soul loses devotion to Mary it is immediately enveloped in darkness, and in that darkness of which the Holy Ghost speaks in the Psalms: " Thou hast appointed darkness, and it is night; in it shall all the beasts of the woods go about." †   When the light of heaven ceases to shine in a soul, all is darkness, and it becomes the haunt of devils and of every sin.   St. Anselm says, that " if any one is disregarded and condemned by Mary, he is necessarily lost," and therefore we may with reason exclaim, " Woe to those who are in opposition to this sun !"   Woe to those who despise its light ! that is to say, all who despise devotion to Mary.

St. Francis Borgia always doubted the perseverance of those in whom he did not find particular devotion to the Blessed Virgin.   On one occasion he questioned some novices as to the saints towards whom they had special devotion, and perceiving some who had it not towards Mary, he instantly warned the master of novices, and desired him to keep a more attentive watch over these unfortunate young men, who all, as he had feared, lost their vocation and renounced the religious state.

It was, then, not without reason that St. Germanus called the most blessed Virgin the breath of Christians; for as the body cannot live without breathing,

* *De Aquæd.*   † Ps. ciii. 20.

so the soul cannot live without having recourse to and recommending itself to Mary, by whose means we certainly acquire and preserve the life of divine grace within our souls. But I will quote the saint's own words: " As breathing is not only a sign but even a cause of life, so the name of Mary, which is constantly found on the lips of God's servants, both proves that they are truly alive, and at the same time causes and preserves their life, and gives them every succor." *

Blessed Allan was one day assaulted by a violent temptation, and was on the point of yielding, for he had not recommended himself to Mary, when the most blessed Virgin appeared to him; and in order that another time he might remember to invoke her aid, she gave him a blow, saying, " If thou hadst recommended thyself to me, thou wouldst not have run into such danger."

On the other hand, Mary says in the following words of the Book of Proverbs, which are applied to her by the Church : " Blessed is the man that heareth me, and that watcheth daily at my gates, and waiteth at the posts of my doors," †—as if she would say, Blessed is he that hears my voice and is constantly attentive to apply at the door of my mercy, and seeks light and help from me. For clients who do this Mary does her part, and obtains them the light and strength they require to abandon sin and walk in the paths of virtue. For this reason Innocent III. beautifully calls her " the moon at night, the dawn at break of day, and the sun at midday." ‡ She is a moon to enlighten those who blindly wander in the night of

* *De Zona Deip.*   † Prov. viii. 34.—*Off. B. V.*
‡ *In Assumpt.* s. 2.

sin, and makes them see and understand the miserable state of damnation in which they are ; she is the dawn (that is, the forerunner of the sun) to those whom she has already enlightened, and makes them abandon sin and return to God, the true sun of justice ; finally, she is a sun to those who are in a state of grace, and prevents them from again falling into the precipice of sin.

Learned writers apply the following words of Ecclesiasticus to Mary : " Her bands are a healthful binding." * " Why bands," asks St. Laurence Justinian, "except it be that she binds her servants, and thus prevents them from straying into the paths of vice ?" † And truly this is the reason for which Mary binds her servants. St. Bonaventure also, in his commentary on the words of Ecclesiasticus, frequently used in the office of Mary, " My abode is in the full assembly of saints," ‡ says that Mary not only has her abode in the full assembly of saints, but also preserves them from falling, keeps a constant watch over their virtue, that it may not fail, and restrains the evil spirits from injuring them. Not only has she her abode in the full assembly of the saints, but she keeps the saints there, by preserving their merits, that they may not lose them, by restraining the devils from injuring them, and by withholding the arm of her Son from falling on sinners. §

In the Book of Proverbs we are told that all Mary's clients are clothed with double garments. " For all her domestics are clothed with double garments." ‖ Cornelius à Lapide explains what this double clothing

---

* Ecclus. vi. 31.   † *De Laud. B. M.* l. 2, p. 3.
‡ Ecclus. xxiv. 16.   § *Spec. B. V. M. lect.* 7.
‖ Prov. xxxi. 21.

is : he says that it " consists in her adorning her faithful servants with the virtues of her Son and with her own," and thus clothed they persevere in virtue.

Therefore St. Philip Neri, in his exhortations to his penitents, used always to say : " My children if you desire perseverance, be devout to our blessed Lady." The Venerable John Berchmans, of the Society of Jesus, used also to say : " Whoever loves Mary will have perseverance." Truly beautiful is the reflection of the Abbot Rupert on this subject in his commentary on the parable of the prodigal son. He says, " That if this dissolute youth had had a mother living, he would never have abandoned the paternal roof, or at least would have returned much sooner than he did ; " meaning thereby that a son of Mary either never abandons God, or, if he has this misfortune, by her help he soon returns.

Oh, did all men but love this most benign and loving Lady, had they but recourse to her always, and without delay, in their temptations, who would fall ? who would ever be lost ? He falls and is lost who has not recourse to Mary. St. Laurence Justinian applies to Mary the words of Ecclesiasticus, " I have walked in the waves of the sea ; " * and makes her say, " I walk with my servants in the midst of the tempests to which they are constantly exposed, to assist and preserve them from falling into sin." †

Bernardine de Bustis relates that a bird was taught to say, " Hail, Mary ! " A hawk was on the point of seizing it, when the bird cried out, " Hail, Mary ! " In an instant the hawk fell dead. God intended to show thereby that if even an irrational creature was pre-

---

* Ecclus. xxiv. 8.   † *De Laud. B. M.* l. 2, p. 1.

served by calling on Mary, how much more would those who are prompt in calling on her when assaulted by devils be delivered from them. We, says St. Thomas of Villanova, need only, when tempted by the devil, imitate little chickens, which, as soon as they perceive the approach of a bird of prey, run under the wings of their mother for protection. This is exactly what we should do whenever we are assaulted by temptation: we should not stay to reason with it, but immediately fly and place ourselves under the mantle of Mary. I will, however, quote the saint's own words addressed to Mary: "As chickens when they see a kite soaring above run and find refuge under the wings of the hen, so are we preserved under the shadow of thy wings. And thou," he continues, "who art our Lady and Mother, hast to defend us; for after God we have no other refuge than thee, who art our only hope and our protectress; towards thee we all turn our eyes with confidence."

Let us, then, conclude in the words of St. Bernard: "O man, whoever thou art, understand that in this world thou art tossed about on a stormy and tempestuous sea, rather than walking on solid ground; remember that if thou wouldst avoid being drowned thou must never turn thine eyes from the brightness of this star, but keep them fixed on it, and call on Mary. In dangers, in straits, in doubts, remember Mary, invoke Mary." Yes, in dangers of sinning, when molested by temptations, when doubtful as to how you should act, remember that Mary can help you; and call upon her, and she will instantly succor you. "Let not her name leave thy lips, let it be ever in thy heart." Your hearts should never lose confidence in her holy name, nor should your lips ever cease to invoke it. "Following her, thou wilt certainly not go astray." Oh, no, if we follow Mary, we shall never err from the paths of salvation. "Imploring her, thou wilt not despair." Each time that we invoke her aid, we shall be inspired with perfect confidence. "If she supports thee, thou canst not fall;" "if she protects thee, thou hast nothing to fear, for thou canst not be lost;" "with her for thy guide, thou wilt not be weary, for thy salvation will be worked out with ease." "If she is propitious, thou wilt gain the port." If Mary undertakes our defence we are certain of gaining the kingdom of heaven. "This do, and thou shalt live."

Prayer.

O compassionate Mother, most sacred Virgin, behold at thy feet the traitor, who, by paying with ingratitude the graces received from God through thy means, has betrayed both thee and Him. But I must tell thee, O most blessed Lady, that my misery, far from taking away my confidence, increases it; for I see that thy compassion is great in proportion to the greatness of my misery. Show thyself, O Mary, full of liberality towards me; for thus thou art towards all who invoke thy aid. All that I ask is that thou shouldst cast thine eyes of compassion on me, and pity me. If thy heart is thus far moved, it cannot do otherwise than protect me; and if thou protectest me, what can I fear? No, I fear nothing, I do not fear my sins, for thou canst provide a remedy; I do not fear devils, for thou art more powerful than the whole of hell; I do not even fear thy Son, though justly irritated against me, for at a word of thine He will be appeased. I only fear lest, in my temptations, and by my own fault, I may cease to recommend myself to thee, and thus be lost. But I now promise thee that I will always have recourse to thee; oh, help me to fulfil my promise. Lose not the opportunity which now presents itself of gratifying thy ardent desire to succor such poor wretches as myself. In thee, O Mother of God, I have unbounded confidence. From thee I hope for grace to bewail my sins as I ought, and from thee I hope for strength never again to fall into them. If I am sick, thou, O heavenly physician, canst heal me. If my sins have weakened me, thy help will strengthen me. O Mary, I hope all from thee; for thou art all-powerful with God. Amen.

III. Mary our Sweetness; she renders Death sweet to her Clients.

" He that is a friend loveth at all times; and a brother is proved in distress," * says the Book of Proverbs. We can never know our friends and relatives in the time of prosperity; it is only in the time of adversity that we see them in their true colors. People of the world never abandon a friend as long as he is in prosperity; but should misfortunes overtake him, and more particularly should he be at the point of death, they immediately forsake him. Mary does not act thus with her clients. In their afflictions, and more particularly in the sorrows of death, the greatest that can be endured in this world, this good Lady and Mother not only does not abandon her faithful servants, but as during our exile she is our life, so also is she at our last hour our sweetness, by obtaining for us a calm and happy death. For from the day on which Mary had the privilege and sorrow of being present at the death of Jesus her Son, Who was the head of all the predestined, it became her privilege to assist also at their deaths. And for this reason the holy Church teaches us to beg this most blessed Virgin to assist us, especially at the moment of death: " Pray for us, sinners, now and at the hour of our death!"

* Prov. xvii. 17.

Oh, how great are the sufferings of the dying ! They suffer from remorse of conscience on account of past sins, from fear of the approaching judgment, and from the uncertainty of their eternal salvation. Then it is that hell arms itself, and spares no efforts to gain the soul which is on the point of entering eternity; for it knows that only a short time remains in which to gain it, and that if it then loses it it has lost it forever. " The devil is come down unto you, having great wrath, knowing that he hath but a short time."* And for this reason the enemy of our salvation, whose charge it was to tempt the soul during life, does not choose at death to be alone, but calls others to his assistance, according to the prophet Isaias: " Their houses shall be filled with serpents."† And indeed they are so; for when a person is at the point of death, the whole place in which he is is filled with devils, who all unite to make him lose his soul.

It is related of St. Andrew Avellino that ten thousand devils came to tempt him at his death. The conflict that he had in his agony with the powers of hell was so terrible that all the good religious who assisted him trembled. They saw the saint's face swelled to such a degree from agitation that it became quite black, every limb trembled and was contorted; his eyes shed a torrent of tears, his head shook violently; all gave evidence of the terrible assault he was enduring on the part of his infernal foes. All wept with compassion, and redoubled their prayers, and at the same time trembled with fear on seeing a saint die thus. They were, however, consoled at seeing that often, as if seeking for help, the saint turned his eyes

* Apoc. xii. 12.   † Is. xiii. 21.

towards a devout picture of Mary; for they remembered that during life he had often said that at death Mary would be his refuge. At length God was pleased to put an end to the contest by granting him a glorious victory; for the contortions of his body ceased, his face resumed its original size and color, and the saint, with his eyes tranquilly fixed on the picture, made a devout inclination to Mary (who it is believed then appeared to him), as if in the act of thanking her, and with a heavenly smile on his countenance tranquilly breathed forth his blessed soul into the arms of Mary. At the same moment a Capuchiness, who was in her agony, turning to the nuns who surrounded her, said, " Recite a Hail Mary; for a saint has just expired."

Ah, how quickly do the rebellious spirits fly from the presence of this Queen! If at the hour of death we have only the protection of Mary, what need we fear from all our infernal enemies? David, fearing the horrors of death, encouraged himself by placing his reliance on the death of the coming Redeemer and on the intercession of the virgin Mother. " For though," he says, " I should walk in the midst of the shadow of death, . . . Thy rod and Thy staff, they have comforted me." *   Cardinal Hugo, explaining these words of the Royal Prophet, says that the staff signifies the cross, and the rod is the intercession of Mary; for she is the rod foretold by the prophet Isaias: " And there shall come forth a rod out of the root of Jesse, and a flower shall rise up out of his root." †   " This divine Mother," says St. Peter Damian, " is that powerful rod with which the violence of the infernal enemies is conquered." ‡   And therefore does St. Antoninus en-

---

* Ps. xxii. 4.   † Is. xi. 1.   ‡ *S. de Assumpt.*

courage us, saying, "If Mary is for us, who shall be against us?"

When Father Emanuel Padial, of the Society of Jesus, was at the point of death, Mary appeared to him, and to console him she said: "See at length the hour is come when the angels congratulate thee, and exclaim: O happy labors, O mortifications well requited! And in the same moment an army of demons was seen taking its flight, and crying out in despair: Alas! we can do naught, for she who is without stain defends him." In like manner, Father Gaspar Haywood was assaulted by devils at his death, and greatly tempted against faith; he immediately recommended himself to the most blessed Virgin, and was heard to exclaim, "I thank thee, Mary; for thou hast come to my aid."*

St. Bonaventure tells us that Mary sends without delay the prince of the heavenly court, St. Michael, with all the angels, to defend her dying servants against the temptations of the devils, and to receive the souls of all who in a special manner and perseveringly have recommended themselves to her. The saint, addressing our blessed Lady, says, "Michael, the leader and prince of the heavenly army, with all the administering spirits, obeys thy commands, O Virgin, and defends and receives the souls of the faithful who have particularly recommended themselves to thee, O Lady, day and night."†

The prophet Isaias tells us that when a man is on the point of leaving the world hell is opened and sends forth its most terrible demons, both to tempt the soul before it leaves the body, and also to accuse

* *Menol.* 28 *Apr.*–9 *Jan.*   † *Spec. B. V. lect.* 3.

it when presented before the tribunal of Jesus Christ
for judgment.   The prophet says, " Hell below was in
an uproar to meet thee at thy coming; it stirred up
the giants for thee." *   But Richard of St. Laurence
remarks that when the soul is defended by Mary the
devils dare not even accuse it, knowing that the Judge
never condemned, and never will condemn, a soul
protected by His august Mother.   He asks, " Who
would dare accuse one who is patronized by the
Mother of Him Who is to judge ? " †   Mary not only
assists her beloved servants at death and encourages
them, but she herself accompanies them to the tribunal seat of God.

As St. Jerome says, writing to the virgin Eustochia,
" What a day of joy will that be for thee, when Mary
the Mother of Our Lord, accompanied by choirs of
virgins, will go to meet thee." ‡   The Blessed Virgin assured St. Bridget of this; for, speaking of her
devout clients at the point of death, she said, " Then
will I, their dear Lady and Mother, fly to them, that
they may have consolation and refreshment." §   St.
Vincent Ferrer says, that not only does the most
blessed Virgin console and refresh them, but that
" she receives the souls of the dying."   This loving
Queen takes them under her mantle, and thus presents
them to the Judge, her Son, and most certainly obtains
their salvation.   This really happened to Charles, the
son of St. Bridget,‖ who died in the army, far from
his mother.   She feared much for his salvation on account of the dangers to which young men are exposed
in a military career; but the Blessed Virgin revealed
to her that he was saved on account of his love for

* Is. xiv. 9.   † *De Laud. V.* l. 2, p. 1.
‡ *De Cust. virg.*   § Rev. l. 1, c. 29.   ‖ Rev. l. 7, c. 13.

her, and that in consequence she herself had assisted
him at death, and had suggested to him the acts that
should be made at that terrible moment. At the same
time the saint saw Jesus on His throne, and the devil
bringing two accusations against the most blessed Virgin: the first was, that Mary had prevented him from
tempting Charles at the moment of death; and the
second was, that the Blessed Virgin had herself presented his soul to the Judge, and so saved it without
even giving him the opportunity of exposing the
grounds on which he claimed it. She then saw the
Judge drive the devil away, and Charles's soul carried
to heaven.

Ecclesiasticus says, that "her bands are a healthful
binding," * and that "in the latter end thou shalt find
rest in her." † Oh, you are indeed fortunate, my
brother, if at death you are bound with the sweet
chains of the love of the Mother of God ! These
chains are chains of salvation; they are chains that
will insure your eternal salvation, and will make you
enjoy in death that blessed peace which will be the
beginning of your eternal peace and rest. Father
Binetti, in his book on the perfections of our blessed
Lord, says, "that having attended the death-bed of a
great lover of Mary, he heard him, before expiring,
utter these words: ' O my father, would that you
could know the happiness that I now enjoy from having served the most holy Mother of God; I cannot
tell you the joy that I now experience.' " ‡ Father
Suarez (in consequence of his devotion to Mary,
which was such that he used to say that he would
willingly exchange all his learning for the merit of a

* Ecclus. vi. 31.　　　† *Ibid.* 29.
‡ *Chef-d'œuvre de D.* p. 3, ch. 6.

single "Hail Mary") died with such peace and joy
that in that moment he said, "I could not have
thought that death was so sweet;" meaning, that he
could never have imagined that it was possible, if he
had not then experienced it, that he could have found
such sweetness in death.

You, devout reader, will, without doubt, experience
the same joy and contentment in death if you can
then remember that you have loved this good Mother,
who cannot be otherwise than faithful to her children
who have been faithful in serving and honoring her,
by their visits, rosaries, and fasts, and still more by
frequently thanking and praising her, and often recommending themselves to her powerful protection.   Nor
will this consolation be withheld, even if you have
been for a time a sinner, provided that, from this day,
you are careful to live well, and to serve this most
gracious and benign Lady.   In your pains, and in the
temptations to despair which the devil will send you,
she will console you, and even come herself to assist
you in your last moments.   St. Peter Damian relates *
that his brother Martin had one day offended God
grievously.   Martin went before an altar of Mary, to
dedicate himself to her as her slave; and for this purpose, and as a mark of servitude, put his girdle round
his neck, and thus addressed her: " My sovereign
Lady, mirror of that purity which I, miserable sinner
that I am, have violated, thereby outraging my God
and thee, I know no better remedy for my crime than
to offer myself to thee for thy slave.   Behold me then:
to thee do I this day dedicate myself, that I may be
thy servant; accept me, though a rebel, and reject me

* *De Bono Suffr.* c, 4.

not." He then left a sum of money on the step of
the altar, and promised to pay a like sum every year,
as a tribute which he owed as a slave of Mary. After
a certain time Martin fell dangerously ill; but one
morning, before expiring, he was heard to exclaim :
" Rise, rise, pay homage to my Queen ! " and then he
added: " And whence is this favor, O Queen of
heaven, that thou shouldst condescend to visit thy
poor servant ? Bless me, O Lady, and permit me not
to be lost, after having honored me with thy presence." At this moment his brother Peter · entered,
and to him he related the visit of Mary, and added
that she had blessed him, but at the same time complained that those who were present had remained
seated in the presence of this great Queen; and
shortly afterwards he sweetly expired in Our Lord.

Such also will be your death, beloved reader, if you
are faithful to Mary. Though you may have hitherto
offended God, she will procure you a sweet and happy
death. And if by chance at that moment you are
greatly alarmed and lose confidence at the sight of
your sins, she will come and encourage you, as she
did Adolphus, Count of Alsace, who abandoned the
world, and embraced the Order of St. Francis. In
the chronicles of that Order we are told that he had
a tender devotion to the Mother of God; and that
when he was at the point of death his former life and
the rigors of divine justice presented themselves before his mind, and caused him to tremble at the
thought of death, and fear for his eternal salvation.
Scarcely had these thoughts entered his mind when
Mary (who is always active when her servants are in
pain), accompanied by many saints, presented herself
before the dying man, and encouraged him with words

of the greatest tenderness, saying: "My own beloved Adolph, thou art mine, thou hast given thyself to me, and now why dost thou fear death so much?" On hearing these words the servant of Mary was instantly relieved, fear was banished from his soul, and he expired in the midst of the greatest peace and joy.

Let us, then, be of good heart, though we be sinners, and feel certain that Mary will come and assist us at death, and comfort and console us with her presence, provided only that we serve her with love during the remainder of the time that we have to be in this world. Our Queen, one day addressing St. Matilda, promised that she would assist all her clients at death who, during their lives, had faithfully served her. "I, as a most tender mother, will faithfully be present at the death of all who piously serve me, and will console and protect them." O God, what a consolation will it be at that last moment of our lives, when our eternal lot has so soon to be decided, to see the Queen of heaven assisting and consoling us with the assurance of her protection.

Besides the cases already given in which we have seen Mary assisting her dying servants there are innumerable others recorded in different works. This favor was granted to St. Clare; to St. Felix, of the Order of Capuchins; to St. Clare of Montefalco; to St. Teresa; to St. Peter of Alcantara. But, for our common consolation, I will relate the following: Father Crasset tells us, that Mary of Oignies saw the Blessed Virgin at the pillow of a devout widow of Willembroc, who was ill with a violent fever. Mary stood by her side, consoling her, and cooling her with a fan. Of St. John of God, who was tenderly devoted to Mary, it is related that he fully expected that she would visit him on his death-bed; but not seeing her arrive, he was afflicted, and perhaps even complained. But when his last hour had come, the divine Mother appeared, and gently reproving him for his little confidence, addressed him in the following tender words, which may well encourage all servants of Mary: " John, it is not in me to forsake my clients at such a moment." As though she had said: " John, of what wast thou thinking? Didst thou imagine I had abandoned thee? And dost thou not know that I never abandon my clients at the hour of death? If I did not come sooner it was that thy time was not yet come; but now that it is come, behold me here to take thee; let us go to heaven." Shortly afterwards the saint expired, and fled to that blessed kingdom, there to thank his most loving Queen for all eternity.

Prayer.

O my most sweet Mother, how shall I die, poor sinner that I am? Even now the thought of that important moment when I must expire, and appear before the judgment-seat of God, and the remembrance that I have myself so often written my condemnation by consenting to sin, makes me tremble. I am confounded, and fear much for my eternal salvation. O Mary, in the blood of Jesus, and in thy intercession, is all my hope. Thou art the Queen of heaven, the mistress of the universe; in short, thou art the Mother of God. Thou art great, but thy greatness does not prevent, nay, even it inclines thee to greater compassion towards us in our miseries. Worldly friends when raised to dignity disdain to notice their former friends who may have fallen into distress. Thy noble and loving heart does not act thus, for the greater the miseries it beholds the greater are its efforts to relieve. Thou, when called upon, dost immediately assist; nay, more, thou dost anticipate our prayers by thy favors; thou consolest us in our afflictions; thou dissipatest the storms by which we are tossed about; thou overcomest all enemies; thou, in fine, never losest an occasion to promote our welfare. May that divine hand which has united in thee such majesty and such tenderness, such greatness and so much love, be forever blessed! I thank my Lord for it, and congratulate myself in having so great an advantage; for truly in thy felicity do I place my own, and I consider thy lot as mine. O comfortress of the afflicted, console a poor creature who recommends himself to thee. The remorse of a conscience overburdened with sins fills me with affliction. I am in doubt as to whether I have sufficiently grieved for them. I see that all my actions are sullied and defective; hell awaits my death in order to accuse me; the outraged justice of God demands satisfaction. My Mother, what will become of me? If thou dost not help me, I am lost. What sayest thou, wilt thou assist me? O compassionate Virgin, console me; obtain for me true sorrow for my sins; obtain for me strength to amend, and to be faithful to God during the rest of my life. And finally, when I am in the last agonies of death, O Mary, my hope, abandon me not; then, more than ever, help and encourage me, that I may not despair at the sight of my sins, which the evil one will then place before me. My Lady, forgive my temerity; come thyself to comfort me with thy presence in that last struggle. This favor thou hast granted to many, grant it also to me. If my boldness is great, thy goodness is greater; for it goes in search of the most miserable to console them. On this I rely. For thy eternal glory, let it be said that thou hast snatched a wretched creature from hell, to which he was already condemned, and that thou hast led him to thy kingdom. Oh, yes, sweet Mother, I hope to have the consolation of remaining always at thy feet in heaven, thanking and blessing and loving thee eternally. O Mary, I shall expect thee at my last hour; deprive me not of this consolation. *Fiat, fiat.* Amen, amen.

MY MOTHER, MY HOPE!

CHAPTER III.

Spes nostra ! salve.

MARY, OUR HOPE.

I. Mary is the Hope of All.

MODERN heretics cannot endure that we should
salute and call Mary our hope: "Hail, our hope!"
They say that God alone is our hope; and that He
curses those who put their trust in creatures in these
words of the prophet Jeremias: "Cursed be the man
that trusteth in man." * Mary, they exclaim, is a
creature; and how can a creature be our hope? This
is what the heretics say; but in spite of this the holy
Church obliges all ecclesiastics and religious each
day to raise their voices, and in name of all the faithful invoke and call Mary by the sweet name of " our
hope," the hope of all.

The angelical doctor St. Thomas says,† that we
can place our hope in a person in two ways: as a
principal cause, and as a mediate one. Those who
hope for a favor from a king hope it from him as
lord; they hope for it from his minister or favorite as
an intercessor. If the favor is granted, it comes pri-
marily from the king, but it comes through the instru-
mentality of the favorite; and in this case he who
seeks the favor is right in calling his intercessor his

* Jer. xvii. 5.   † 2. 2, q. 25, a. 1, ad 3.

hope. The King of heaven, being infinite goodness, desires in the highest degree to enrich us with His graces; but because confidence is requisite on our part, and in order to increase it in us, He has given us His own Mother to be our Mother and advocate, and to her He has given all power to help us; and therefore He wills that we should repose our hope of salvation and of every blessing in her. Those who place their hopes in creatures alone, independently of God, as sinners do, and in order to obtain the friend-ship and favor of a man fear not to outrage His divine majesty, are most certainly cursed by God, as the prophet Jeremias says. But those who hope in Mary, as Mother of God, who is able to obtain graces and eternal life for them, are truly blessed and accept-able to the heart of God, Who desires to see that greatest of His creatures honored; for she loved and honored Him in this world more than all men and angels put together. And therefore we justly and reasonably call the Blessed Virgin our hope, trusting, as Cardinal Bellarmine says, "that we shall obtain through her intercession that which we should not obtain by our own unaided prayers." "We pray to her," says the learned Suarez, "in order that the dig-nity of the intercessor may supply for our own un-worthiness; so that," he continues, "to implore the Blessed Virgin in such a spirit is not diffidence in the mercy of God, but fear of our own unworthiness." *

It is, then, not without reason that the holy Church, in the words of Ecclesiasticus, calls Mary "the Mother of holy hope."† She is the Mother who gives birth to holy hope in our hearts; not to the hope of the

---

* *De Inc.* p. 2, d. 23, s. 3.   † Ecclus. xxiv. 24.

vain and transitory goods of this life, but of the immense and eternal goods of heaven.

"Hail, then, O hope of my soul!" exclaims St. Ephrem, addressing this divine Mother; "hail, O certain salvation of Christians; hail, O helper of sinners; hail, fortress of the faithful and salvation of the world!"* Other saints remind us, that after God our only hope is Mary; and therefore they call her, "after God, their only hope."†

St. Ephrem, reflecting on the present order of Providence, by which God wills (as St. Bernard says, and as we shall prove at length) that all who are saved should be saved by the means of Mary, thus addresses her: "O Lady, cease not to watch over us; preserve and guard us under the wings of thy compassion and mercy, for, after God, we have no hope but in thee."‡ St. Thomas of Villanova repeats the same thing, calling her "our only refuge, help, and asylum."§ St. Bernard seems to give the reason for this when he says, "See, O man, the designs of God—designs by which He is able to dispense His mercy more abundantly to us; for, desiring to redeem the whole human race, He has placed the whole price of redemption in the hands of Mary, that she may dispense it at will." ‖

In the Book of Exodus we read that God commanded Moses to make a mercy-seat of the purest gold, because it was thence that He would speak to him. "Thou shalt make also a propitiatory of the purest gold. . . . Thence will I give orders, and will speak to thee."¶ St. Andrew of Crete says that "the

---

* *De Laud. Dei Gen.*
‡ *De Laud. Dei Gen.*
‖ *De Aquæd.*

† *Cant. p. Psalt.*
§ *In Nat. B. V. Conc.* 3.
¶ Exod. xxv. 17.

whole world embraces Mary as being this propitiatory." And commenting on his words a pious author
exclaims, " Thou, O Mary, art the propitiatory of the
whole world. From thee does our most compassionate Lord speak to our hearts; from thee He speaks
words of pardon and mercy; from thee He bestows Hi
gifts; from thee all good flows to us." * And therefore, before the Divine Word took flesh in the womb
of Mary, He sent an archangel to ask her consent:
because He willed that the world should receive the
Incarnate Word through her, and that she should be
the source of every good. Hence St. Irenæus remarks, that as Eve was seduced by a fallen angel to
flee from God, so Mary was led to receive God into
her womb, obeying a good angel ; and thus by her
obedience repaired Eve's disobedience, and became
her advocate, and that of the whole human race. " If
Eve disobeyed God, yet Mary was persuaded to obey
God, that the Virgin Mary might become the advocate of the virgin Eve. And as the human race was
bound to death through a virgin, it is saved through a
virgin." † And Blessed Raymond Jordano also says,
" that every good, every help, every grace that men
have received and will receive from God until the
end of time, came, and will come, to them by the intercession and through the hands of Mary." ‡

The devout Blosius, then, might well exclaim, " O
Mary, O thou who art so loving and gracious towards
all who love thee, tell me, who can be so infatuated
and unfortunate as not to love thee ? Thou, in the
midst of their doubts and difficulties, enlightenest the

* *Paciucch. in Sal. Ang. Exc.* 20.
† *Ap. C. à Lap. In Prov.* xxxi. 29.
‡ *Cont. B. M. in. prol.*

minds of all who, in their afflictions, have recourse to
thee. Thou encouragest those who fly to thee in time
of danger; thou succorest those who call upon thee;
thou, after thy divine Son, art the certain salvation of
thy faithful servants. Hail, then, O hope of those who
are in despair; O succor of those who are abandoned.
O Mary, thou art all-powerful; for thy divine Son, to
honor thee, complies instantly with all thy desires." *

St. Germanus, recognizing in Mary the source of all
our good, and that she delivers us from every evil, thus
invokes her: " O my sovereign Lady, thou àlone art
the one whom God has appointed to be my solace here
below; thou art the guide of my pilgrimage, the
strength of my weakness, the riches of my poverty, the
remedy for the healing of my wounds, the soother of
my pains, the end of my captivity, the hope of my salvation! Hear my prayers, have pity on my tears, I
conjure thee, O thou who art my queen, my refuge,
my love, my help, my hope, and my strength." †

We need not, then, be surprised that St. Antoninus
applies the following verse of the Book of Wisdom to
Mary: " Now all good things came to me together with
her." ‡ For as this Blessed Virgin is the Mother and
dispenser of all good things, the whole world, and
more particularly each individual who lives in it as a
devout client of this great Queen, may say with truth,
that with devotion to Mary both he and the world
have obtained everything good and perfect. The saint
thus expresses his thought: " She is the Mother of all
good things, and the world can truly say, that with her
(that is, the most blessed Virgin) it has received all
good things." § And hence the blessed Abbot of Celles

* *Par. an.* p. 2, c. 4.   † *Encom. in S. Deip.*
‡ Wis. vii. 11.   § P. 4, l. 15, c. 20, § 12.

expressly declares, "that when we find Mary, we find all." * Whoever finds Mary finds every good thing, obtains all graces and all virtues; for by her powerful intercession she obtains all that is necessary to enrich him with divine grace. In the Book of Proverbs Mary herself tells us that she possesses all the riches of God, that is to say, His mercies, that she may dispense them in favor of her lovers: "With me are riches . . . and glorious riches . . . that I may enrich them that love me." † And therefore St. Bonaventure says, "that we ought all to keep our eyes constantly fixed on Mary's hands, that through them we may receive the graces that we desire." ‡

Oh, how many who were once proud have become humble by devotion to Mary! how many who were passionate have become meek ! how many in the midst of darkness have found light ! how many who were in despair have found confidence ! how many who were lost have found salvation by the same powerful means! And this she clearly foretold in the house of Elizabeth, in her own sublime canticle: "Behold, from henceforth all generations shall call me blessed." And St. Bernard, interpreting her words, says: "All generations call thee blessed, because thou hast given life and glory to all nations,§ for in thee sinners find pardon, and the just perseverance in the grace of God." ∥

Hence the devout Lanspergius makes Our Lord thus address the world: "Men, poor children of Adam, who live surrounded by so many enemies, and in the midst of so many trials, endeavor to honor My Mother and yours in a special manner: for I have given Mary to the world that she may be your model,

---

* *De Cont. de V. M. in Prol.*   † Prov. viii. 18.
‡ *Spec. B. V. lect.* 3.   § *In Pentec.* s. 2,   ∥ *In Pent.* s. 2.

and that from her you may learn to lead good lives;
and also that she may be a refuge to which you can
fly in all your afflictions and trials.   I have rendered
this, my daughter, such that no one need fear or have
the least repugnance to have recourse to her; and for
this purpose I have created her of so benign and compassionate a disposition that she knows not how to despise any one who takes refuge with her, nor can she
deny her favor to any one who seeks it.   The mantle
of her mercy is open to all, and she allows no one
to leave her feet without consoling him." *   May the
immense goodness of our God be ever praised and
blessed for having given us so great, so tender, so
loving a Mother and advocate.

O God, how tender are the sentiments of confidence
expressed by the enamoured St. Bonaventure towards
Jesus our most loving Redeemer, and Mary our most
loving advocate !   He says, " Whatever God foresees
to be my lot, I know that He cannot refuse Himself
to any one who loves Him and seeks for Him with his
whole heart.   I will embrace Him with my love; and
if He does not bless me, I will still cling to Him so
closely that He will be unable to go without me.   If I
can do nothing else, at least I will hide myself in His
wounds, and taking up my dwelling there, it will be in
Himself alone that He will find me."   And the saint
concludes, " If my Redeemer rejects me on account of
my sins, and drives me from His sacred feet, I will cast
myself at those of His beloved Mother Mary, and there
I will remain prostrate until she has obtained my forgiveness; for this Mother of mercy knows not, and has
never known, how to do otherwise than compassionate

* *Alloq.* l. i, p. 4, *can.*12.

the miserable, and comply with the desires of the most
destitute who fly to her for succor; and therefore," he
says, " if not by duty, at least by compassion, she will
engage her Son to pardon me." *

" Look down upon us, then," let us exclaim, in the
words of Euthymius, "look down upon us, O most
compassionate Mother; cast thine eyes of mercy on
us, for we are thy servants, and in thee we have placed
all our confidence." †

Prayer.

O Mother of holy love, our life, our refuge, and our
hope, thou well knowest that thy Son Jesus Christ, not
content with being Himself our perpetual advocate with
the Eternal Father, has willed that thou also shouldst
interest thyself with Him, in order to obtain the divine
mercies for us. He has decreed that thy prayers should
aid our salvation, and has made them so efficacious that
they obtain all that they ask. To thee therefore, who art
the hope of the miserable, do I, a wretched sinner, turn
my eyes. I trust, O Lady, that in the first place through
the merits of Jesus Christ, and then through thy intercession, I shall be saved. Of this I am certain ; and my
confidence in thee is such that if my eternal salvation
were in my own hands I should place it in thine, for I
rely more on thy mercy and protection than on all my
own works. My Mother and my hope, abandon me not,
though I deserve that thou shouldst do so. See my
miseries, and, being moved thereby with compassion,
help and save me. I own that I have too often closed
my heart, by my sins, against the lights and helps that
thou hast procured for me from the Lord. But thy compassion for the miserable, and thy power with God, far

---

* *Stim. div. am.* p. 3, c. 13.   † *Ap. Sur.* 31 *Aug.*

surpass the number and malice of my sins. It is well known to all, both in heaven and on earth, that whosoever is protected by thee is certainly saved. All may forget me, provided only that thou dost remember me, O Mother of an omnipotent God. Tell Him that I am thy servant; say only that thou defendest me, and I shall be saved. O Mary, I trust in thee; in this hope I live; in it I desire and hope to die, repeating always, "Jesus is my only hope, and after Jesus the most blessed Virgin Mary."

II. Mary is the Hope of Sinners.

In the first chapter of the Book of Genesis we read that "God made two great lights; a greater light to rule the day, and a lesser light to rule the night." * Cardinal Hugo says that "Christ is the greater light to rule the just, and Mary the lesser to rule sinners;" meaning that the sun is a figure of Jesus Christ, Whose light is enjoyed by the just who live in the clear day of divine grace; and that the moon is a figure of Mary, by whose means those who are in the night of sin are enlightened. Since Mary is this auspicious luminary, and is so for the benefit of poor sinners, should any one have been so unfortunate as to fall into the night of sin, what is he to do? Innocent III. replies, "Whoever is in the night of sin, let him cast his eyes on the moon, let him implore Mary." † Since he has lost the light of the sun of justice by losing the grace of God, let him turn to the moon, and beseech Mary; and she will certainly give him light to see the misery of his state, and strength to leave it without delay. St. Methodius says "that by

* Gen. i. 16.   † *In Assumpt.* s. 2.

the prayers of Mary almost innumerable sinners are converted." *

One of the titles which is the most encouraging to poor sinners, and under which the Church teaches us to invoke Mary in the Litany of Loretto, is that of "refuge of sinners." In Judea in ancient times there were cities of refuge, in which criminals who fled there for protection were exempt from the punishments which they had deserved. Nowadays these cities are not so numerous; there is but one, and that is Mary, of whom the psalmist says, " Glorious things are said of thee, O city of God." † But this city differs from the ancient ones in this respect—that in the latter all kinds of criminals did not find refuge, nor was the protection extended to every class of crime; but under the mantle of Mary all sinners, without exception, find refuge for every sin that they may have committed, provided only that they go there to seek for this protection. " I am the city of refuge," says St. John Damascene, in the name of our Queen, " to all who fly to me." ‡ And it is sufficient to have recourse to her, for whoever has the good fortune to enter this city need not speak to be saved. " Assemble yourselves, and let us enter into the fenced city, and let us be silent there," § to speak in the words of the prophet Jeremias. This city, says Blessed Albert the Great, is the most holy Virgin fenced in with grace and glory. " And let us be silent there," that is, continues an interpreter, " because we dare not invoke the Lord, Whom we have offended; she will invoke and ask." ‖ For if we do not presume to ask

---

* *Paciucch. in Ps.* lxxxvi. *exc.* 17. † Ps. lxxxvi. 3.
‡ *In Dorm. B. V. or.* 2. § Jer. viii. 14.
‖ *Bib. Mar. Jer.* n. 3.

Our Lord to forgive us, it will suffice to enter this
city and be silent, for Mary will speak and ask all that
we require.   And for this reason a devout author exhorts all sinners to take refuge under the mantle of
Mary, exclaiming, " Fly, O Adam and Eve, and all
you their children who have outraged God—fly, and
take refuge in the bosom of this good Mother; know
you not that she is our only city of refuge ? " * " the
only hope of sinners," † as she is also called in a sermon by an ancient writer, found in the works of St.
Augustine.

St. Ephrem, addressing the Blessed Virgin, says,
" Thou art the only advocate of sinners, and of all
who are unprotected."   And then he salutes her in
the following words: " Hail, refuge and hospital of
sinners ! " ‡—true refuge, in which alone they can
hope for reception and liberty.   And an author remarks that this was the meaning of David when he
said, " For He hath hidden me in His tabernacle." §
And truly what can this tabernacle of God be, unless
it is Mary ? who is called by St. Germanus, " A tabernacle made by God, in which He alone entered to ac-
complish the great work of the redemption of man." ‖

St. Basil of Seleucia remarks, " that if God granted
to some who were only His servants such power that
not only their touch but even their shadows healed
the sick, who were placed for this purpose in the public streets, how much greater power must we suppose
that He has granted to her who was not only His
handmaid but His Mother ? "   We may indeed say
that Our Lord has given us Mary as a public infirm-

* *B. Fernandez in Gen.* c. 3, s. 22.
† *Serm.* 194, *E. B. app.*   ‡ *De Laud. Dei gen.*
§ Ps.·xxvi. 5.   ‖ *In Nat. S. M. or.* 2.

ary, in which all who are sick, poor, and destitute can be received. But now I ask, in hospitals erected expressly for the poor, who have the greatest claim to admission ? Certainly the most infirm, and those who are in the greatest need.

And for this reason should any one find himself devoid of merit and overwhelmed with spiritual infirmities, that is to say, sin, he can thus address Mary: O Lady, thou art the refuge of the sick poor; reject me not; for as I am the poorest and the most infirm of all, I have the greatest right to be welcomed by thee.

Let us then cry out with St. Thomas of Villanova, " O Mary, we poor sinners know no other refuge than thee, for thou art our only hope, and on thee we rely for our salvation." * Thou art our only advocate with Jesus Christ; to thee we all turn ourselves.

In the revelations of St. Bridget Mary is called the "star preceding the sun," † giving us thereby to understand that when devotion towards the divine Mother begins to manifest itself in a soul that is in a state of sin it is a certain mark that before long God will enrich it with His grace. The glorious St. Bonaventure, in order to revive the confidence of sinners in the protection of Mary, places before them the picture of a tempestuous sea, into which sinners have already fallen from the ship of divine grace; they are already dashed about on every side by remorse of conscience and by fear of the judgments of God ; they are without light or guide, and are on the point of losing the last breath of hope and falling into despair; then it is that Our Lord, pointing out Mary to them, who is commonly called the " star of the sea,"

* *De Nat. V. M. conc.* 3.   † *Rev. Extr.* c. 50.

raises His voice and says, " O poor lost sinners, despair not; raise up your eyes, and cast them on this
beautiful star; breathe again with confidence, for it
will save you from this tempest, and will guide you
into the port of salvation."* St. Bernard says the
same thing: " If thou wouldst not be lost in the tempest, cast thine eyes on the star, and invoke Mary." †

The devout Blosius declares that " she is the only
refuge of those who have offended God, the asylum
of all who are oppressed by temptation, calamity, or
persecution. This Mother is all mercy, benignity,
and sweetness, not only to the just, but also to de-
spairing sinners; so that no sooner does she perceive
them coming to her, and seeking her health from their
hearts, than she aids them, welcomes them, and obtains their pardon from her Son. She knows not how
to despise any one, however unworthy he may be of
mercy, and therefore denies her protection to none; she
consoles all, and is no sooner called upon than she
helps whoever it may be that invokes her. She by her
sweetness often awakens and draws sinners to her devotion who are the most at enmity with God and the
most deeply plunged in the lethargy of sin; and then,
by the same means, she excites them effectually, and
prepares them for grace, and thus renders them fit for
the kingdom of heaven. God has created this His
beloved daughter of so compassionate and sweet a
disposition that no one can fear to have recourse to
her." The pious author concludes in these words:
" It is impossible for any one to perish who atten-
tively, and with humility, cultivates devotion towards
this divine Mother." ‡

* *Psal. B. V. ps.* 18.   † *De Laud. V. M. hom.* 2.
‡ *Par. an. fid.* p. 1, c. 18.

In Ecclesiasticus Mary is called a plane-tree: " As
a plane-tree I was exalted."* And she is so called
that sinners may understand that as the plane-tree
gives shelter to travellers from the heat of the sun, so
does Mary invite them to take shelter under her protection from the wrath of God, justly enkindled against
them. St. Bonaventure remarks that the prophet
Isaias complained of the times in which he lived, saying, " Behold Thou art angry, and we have sinned; . . .
there is none . . . that riseth up and taketh hold of
Thee."† And then he makes the following commentary: " It is true, O Lord, that at the time there was
none to raise up sinners, and withhold Thy wrath, for
Mary was not yet born;" " before Mary," to quote the
saint's own words, " there was no one who could thus
dare to restrain the arm of God." But now, if God
is angry with a sinner, and Mary takes him under her
protection, she withholds the avenging arm of her Son,
and saves him. "And so," continues the same saint,
" no one can be found more fit for this office than
Mary, who seizes the sword of divine justice with her
own hands to prevent it from falling upon and punish-
ing the sinner." ‡ Upon the same subject Richard of
St. Laurence says that " God, before the birth of Mary,
complained by the mouth of the prophet Ezechiel
that there was no one to rise up and withhold Him
from chastising sinners, but that He could find no one,
for this office was reserved for our blessed Lady, who
withholds His arm until He is pacified."§

Basil of Seleucia encourages sinners, saying, " O
sinner, be not discouraged, but have recourse to Mary
in all thy necessities; call her to thine assistance, for

---

* Ecclus. xxiv. 19.   † Is. lxiv. 5.
‡ *Spec. B. V. lect.* 7, 14.   § *De Laud. B. M.* l. 2, p. 5.

thou wilt always find her ready to help thee; for such is the divine will that she should help all in every kind of necessity."* This Mother of mercy has so great a desire to save the most abandoned sinners that she herself goes in search of them, in order to help them; and if they have recourse to her, she knows how to find the means to render them acceptable to God. The patriarch Isaac, desiring to eat of some wild animal, promised his blessing to his son Esau on his procuring this food for him; but Rebecca, who was anxious that her other son Jacob should receive the blessing, called him and said, "Go thy way to the flock, bring me two kids of the best, that I may make of them meat for thy father, such as he gladly eateth."† St. Antoninus says, ‡ "that Rebecca was a figure of Mary, who commands the angels to bring her sinners (meant by kids), that she may adorn them in such a way (by obtaining for them sorrow and purpose of amendment) as to render them dear and acceptable to the Lord." And here we may well apply to our blessed Lady the words of the Abbot Franco: "O truly sagacious woman, who so well knew how to dress these kids that not only are they equal to, but often superior in flavor to, real venison." §

The Blessed Virgin herself revealed to St. Bridget " that there is no sinner in the world, however much he may be at enmity with God, who does not return to Him and recover His grace, if he has recourse to her and asks her assistance." ‖ The same St. Bridget one day heard Jesus Christ address His Mother, and say that "she would be ready to obtain the grace of God

* *Paciucch. in Salve R. exc.* 7.
† Gen. xxvii. 9.   ‡ P. 4, t. 15, c. 2, § 2.
§ *De Grat. D.* l. 3.   ‖ Rev. l. 6, c. 10.

for Lucifer himself, if only he humbled himself so far
as to seek her aid." * That proud spirit will never
himself so far as to implore the protection of Mary;
but if such a thing were possible, Mary would be sufficiently compassionate, and her prayers would have
sufficient power, to obtain both forgiveness and salvation for him from God. But that which cannot be
verified with regard to the devil is verified in the case
of sinners who have recourse to this compassionate
Mother.

Noe's ark was a true figure of Mary; for as in it all
kinds of beasts were saved, so under the mantle of
Mary all sinners, who by their vices and sensuality are
already like beasts, find refuge; but with this differ-
ence, as a pious author remarks, that " while the brutes
that entered the ark remained brutes, the wolf remaining a wolf, and a tiger a tiger—under the mantle
of Mary, on the other hand, the wolf becomes a lamb,
and the tiger a dove." † One day St. Gertrude saw
Mary with her mantle open, and under it there were
many wild beasts of different kinds—leopards, lions,
and bears; and she saw that not only our blessed
Lady did not drive them away, but that she welcomed
and caressed them with her benign hand. The saint
understood that these wild beasts were miserable sinners, who are welcomed by Mary with sweetness and
love the moment they have recourse to her. ‡

It was, then, not without reason that St. Bernard
addressed the Blessed Virgin, saying, " Thou, O Lady,
dost not reject any sinner who approaches thee, however loathsome and repugnant he may be. If he asks
thy assistance, thou dost not disdain to extend thy

* *Rev. extr.* c. 50.
† *Paciucch. in Sal. Ang. exc.* 4.   ‡ *Insin.* l. 4, c. 50.

compassionate hand to him, to extricate him from the gulf of despair." *   May our God be eternally blessed and thanked, O most amiable Mary, for having created thee so sweet and benign, even towards the most miserable sinners!   Truly unfortunate is he who loves thee not, and who, having it in his power to obtain thy assistance, has no confidence in thee.   He who has not recourse to Mary is lost; but who was ever lost that had recourse to the most blessed Virgin?

It is related in the Sacred Scriptures that Booz allowed Ruth "to gather the ears of corn after the reapers." †   St. Bonaventure says, " that as Ruth found favor with Booz, so has Mary found favor with Our Lord, and is also allowed to gather the ears of corn after the reapers.   The reapers followed by Mary are all evangelical laborers, missionaries, preachers, and confessors, who are constantly reaping souls for God.   But there are some hardened and rebellious souls which are abandoned even by these.   To Mary alone it is granted to save them by her powerful intercession." ‡   Truly unfortunate are they if they do not allow themselves to be gathered, even by this sweet Lady.   They will indeed be most certainly lost and accursed.   But, on the other hand, blessed is he who has recourse to this good Mother.   "There is not in the world," says the devout Blosius, " any sinner, however revolting and wicked, who is despised or rejected by Mary; she can, she wills, and she knows how to reconcile him to her most beloved Son, if only he will seek her assistance." §

With reason then, O my most sweet Queen, did St. John Damascene salute and call thee the " hope of

---

* *Depr. ad B. V.*   † Ruth ii. 3.

‡ *Spec. B. V. M. lect.* 5.   § *Sac. an. fid.* p. 3, c. 5.

those who are in despair." With reason did St. Laurence Justinian call thee " the hope of malefactors," and another ancient writer " the only hope of sinners." St. Ephrem calls her " the safe harbor of all sailing on the sea of the world." This last-named saint also calls her " the consolation of those who are to be condemned." With reason, finally, does St. Bernard exhort even the desperate not to despair; and, full of joy and tenderness towards his most dear Mother, he lovingly exclaims: "And who, O Lady, can be without confidence in thee, since thou assistest even those who are in despair ? And I doubt not that whenever we have recourse to thee we shall obtain all that we desire. Let him, then, who is without hope, hope in thee."*
St. Antoninus relates † that there was a sinner who was at enmity with God, and who had a vision in which he found himself before the dread tribunal; the devil accused him, and Mary defended him. The enemy produced the catalogue of his sins; it was thrown into the scales of divine justice, and weighed far more than all his good works. But then his great advocate, extending her sweet hand, placed it on the balance, and so caused it to turn in favor of her client; giving him thereby to understand that she would obtain his pardon if he changed his life; and this he did after the vision, and was entirely converted.

Prayer.

O most pure Virgin Mary, I venerate thy most holy heart, which was the delight and resting place of God, thy heart overflowing with humility, purity, and divine love. I, an unhappy sinner, approach thee with a heart

---

* *Med. in Salv. R.* † P. 4, t. 15, c. 5, § 1.

all loathsome and wounded.   O compassionate Mother, disdain me not on this account; let such a sight rather move thee to greater tenderness, and excite thee to help me.   Do not stay to seek virtues or merit in me before assisting me.   I am lost, and the only thing I merit is hell.   See only my confidence in thee and the purpose I have to amend.   Consider all that Jesus has done and suffered for me, and then abandon me if thou canst.   I offer thee all the pains of His life; the cold that He endured in the stable; His journey into Egypt; the blood which He shed; the poverty, sweats, sorrows, and death that He endured for me; and this in thy presence.   For the love of Jesus, take charge of my salvation.   Ah, my Mother, I will not and cannot fear that thou wilt reject me, now that I have recourse to thee and ask thy help. Did I fear this, I should be offering an outrage to thy mercy, which goes in quest of the wretched, in order to help them.   O Lady, deny not thy compassion to one to whom Jesus has not denied His blood.   But the merits of this blood will not be applied to me unless thou recommendest me to God.   Through thee do I hope for salvation.   I ask not for riches, honors, or earthly goods. I seek only the grace of God, love towards thy Son, the accomplishment of His will, and His heavenly kingdom, that I may love Him eternally.   Is it possible that thou wilt not hear me?   No; for already thou hast granted my prayer, as I hope; already thou prayest for me; already thou obtainest me the graces that I ask; already thou takest me under thy protection.   My Mother, abandon me not.   Never, never cease to pray for me, until thou seest me safe in heaven at thy feet, blessing and thanking thee forever.   Amen.

And thus Father Suarez concludes, that it is the sentiment of the universal Church, " that the intercession and prayers of Mary are, above those of all others, not only useful, but necessary." * Necessary, in accordance with what we have already said, not with an absolute necessity; for the mediation of Jesus Christ alone is absolutely necessary; but with a moral necessity; for the Church believes with St. Bernard, that God has determined that no grace shall be granted otherwise than by the hands of Mary. " God wills," says the saint, " that we should have nothing that has not passed through the hands of Mary ;" † and before St. Bernard, St. Ildephonsus asserted the same thing, addressing the Blessed Virgin in the following terms : " O Mary, God has decided on committing all good gifts that He has provided for men to thy hands, and therefore He has intrusted all treasures and riches of grace to thee." ‡ And therefore St. Peter Damian remarks, " that God would not become man without the consent of Mary ; in the first place, that we might feel ourselves under great obligations to her ; and in the second, that we might understand that the salvation of all is left to the care of the Blessed Virgin." §

* *De Inc.* p. 2, d. 23, s. 3.
† *In Vig. Nat. D.* s. 3.　　　　‡ *In Cor. Virg.* c. 15.
§ *Paciucch. in Ps.* lxxxvi. *exc.* 1.

Hail, Mary, full of grace, the Lord is with thee. Blessed art thou amongst women and blessed is the fruit of thy womb, Jesus. Holy Mary, Mother of God, pray for us sinners, now and at the hour of our death. Amen.

If you have enjoyed this book, consider making your next selection from among the following . . .